Bonnie Odonnell
601 N Hathaway St
Winamac IN 46996-1017

Oct. 12, 2007

EveryDay Spelling

Laurie Rozakis, Ph.D.

MADISON
PARK
PRESS™

NEW YORK

Published by Madison Park Press, 15 East 26th Street, New York, NY 10010. Madison Park Press is a trademark of Bookspan.

Book design by Pearl Lau

ISBN: 978-1-58288-283-3

Printed in the United States of America

TABLE OF CONTENTS

• • • •

NTRODUCTION

Still smarting from the way you misspelled *tariff* in the fourth-grade spelling bee? Glad you got married so you don't have to spell *bachelor* again? Know you graduated from college but can never remember if you're an *alumnus* or an *alumna*? Do you consider a computer spell checker the best thing since sliced bread (even though a spell checker can't help with homonyms and other tricky words)? Then this book is for you.

Let me say right off the bat that there is little evidence to suggest that spelling aptitude has anything to do with basic intelligence. Some of the world's sharpest people are lousy spellers. As my elementary school friends will confirm, I mangled most spelling words well into junior high. My favorite was shiny (*shiney, shinny,* etc.), but, like Vice-President Dan Quayle, I did some pretty rude things to *potato,* too. Furthermore, many people are behind the eightball because they have learning disabilities—often undiagnosed and thus unknown to even themselves—that make spelling a truly difficult and frustrating problem.

Excusable or not, it's worth the time and trouble it takes to overcome poor spelling. It's like being poorly dressed or pressed. You wouldn't go out looking like you slept in your suit. (Okay, so maybe you would, but I don't want to go there.) How could you warp words?

So what if you never read the letters in your alphabet soup? So what if attention to detail isn't your strong suit? You can still learn to spell like a pro. Hey, I did, and I still can't program a VCR, complete a withdrawal from an ATM, or make my kids understand the meaning of "No." But I learned how to spell—and so can you. Work your way through the lessons in this book and you'll feel a great deal more confident when it comes to expressing yourself in writing.

SPELLING **IS** IMPORTANT. THE WORD **SPELL**
ITSELF UNDERSCORES THIS IMPORTANCE. IT
DERIVES FROM THE MIDDLE ENGLISH WORD
SPELLEN, WHICH MEANS "TO READ OUT."
THE WORD **SPELLING** IS RELATED TO AN OLD
ENGLISH WORD
MEANING "TO TALK."

BEE A GOOD SPELLER

Can you spell? Take this pretest to see how well you spell. Use what you learn here to focus on the sections of this book that you need the most.

In each of the following groups of words, only one of the words is mis-spelled. Select the misspelled word and write it correctly in the space provided.

1. aguering.........knives.........shepherd.........thousandth

2. baggy.........unreleived.........canine.........vengeful

3. contagious.........obituary.........lonliness.........cadence

4. millinery.........sacrafice.........caramel.........burglarize

5. publicity.........promontory.........sieze.........patriarch

6. bridle.........loosely.........breakage.........symtom

7. civillian.........primeval.........apologetic.........truancy

8. uncanny.........statuesque.........ajournment.........aisle

9. trigonometry.........exhaust.........Artic.........visualize

10. bewitches.........satchel.........vegetable.........obstinite

11. dissaprove.........perpetuate.........veterinarian.........transferable

12. colleague.........surpise.........preliminary.........wiry

13. mispell.........familiar.........ceiling.........diploma

14. fiend.........mannerism.........diagnosis.........sking

15. incidentally.........original.........bravly.........farce

16. probably.........magnificent.........fervor.........benefitted

17. conceled.........almond.........vocal.........adrenaline

18. Britian.........wholly.........narrative.........friendliness

19. bookeeper.........medicine.........wholesome.........conspicuous

20. ginham.........exercise.........witness.........president

✔ SCORE YOURSELF

16–20 correct:	You can proofread my work anytime.
11–5 correct:	You'll be okay with a good spell checker.
6–10 correct:	You're treading on thin ice.
0–5 correct:	You need me, you really need me.

ANSWERS

1. arguing	8. adjournment	15. bravely
2. unrelieved	9. Arctic	16. benefited
3. loneliness	10. obstinate	17. concealed
4. sacrifice	11. disapprove	18. Britain
5. seize	12. surprise	19. bookkeeper
6. symptom	13. misspell	20. gingham
7. civilian	14. skiing	

THE ROMAN ALPHABET HAS ALWAYS BEEN INADEQUATE FOR THE PHONETIC REPRESENTATION OF THE ENGLISH LANGUAGE, MOST STRIKINGLY SO FOR MODERN ENGLISH. FOR EXAMPLE, WE HAVE ONLY FIVE VOWELS—A,E,I,O,U. THAT THIS NUMBER OF VOWELS IS INSUFFICIENT IS INDICATED BY THE FACT THAT THE FIRST OF THESE ALONE MAY HAVE AS MANY AS SIX DIFFERENT SOUND VALUES, AS IN CAT, CAME, CALM, ANY, CALL, AND WAS.

PART 1:

SPELLING TIPS

● ● ● ●

"Waiter, waiter!" cried the irate patron in the fancy restaurant. "What's this fly doing in my soup?"

"Looks like the backstroke to me," replied the waiter.

Right or wrong, good or bad, you know that spelling matters. A fly in your soup doesn't do much for your appetite; likewise, a misspelled word can destroy the effect of an entire document. In the first section of this book, you'll learn some effective and fun ways to learn to spell.

CHAPTER 1

*T*RICKS OF THE TRADE

YOU MUST REMEMBER THIS

Have to spell a quirky word? Don't panic! Instead, try some easy tricks of the spelling trade. This chapter covers a dozen nifty ones. Here they are:

1. Pronounce the word correctly.

2. Classify errors.

3. Break the word into smaller parts that you can spell easily.

4. Use print dictionaries and computer spell checkers.

5. Air write.

6. Guess and check.

7. Practice with word cards.

8. Visualize the correct spelling.

9. Learn and create mnemonics (memory games).

10. Use spelling rules.

11. Know word families.

12. Make sure you have the word you really want.

ALL THE RIGHT MOVES

There are so many tried-and-true spelling techniques that you're sure to find a few that work for you.

Why don't we simply spell words the way they sound? You're not the first smart person to ask that question. In the year 1200, a monk named Orm developed a phonetic spelling system. It didn't catch on, but that didn't stop others from following in his footsteps (in spelling, not monkhood).

Among those who tried to overhaul our spelling system were Benjamin Franklin, Theodore Roosevelt, George Bernard Shaw, and Upton Sinclair.

In *The Devil's Dictionary*, writer and wit Ambrose Bierce defines *orthography* as "the science of spelling by the eye instead of the ear. Advocated with more heat than light by the inmates of every asylum for the insane." So why haven't we gotten around to reforming spelling to bridge the chasm between *phonology* (the way we say words) and *orthography* (the way we write them)? And while we're at it, why haven't we worked out the kinks with Olestra, fixed the ozone layer, and found the Fountain of Youth?

Here are some reasons why our spelling remains the way it is:

- Uniform spelling would rob English of its rich legacy of *homophones*.
- We'd also lose the fascinating and useful etymological history of many words.
- Creating a unified system of spelling is a job for Superman, and he's busy with evil Lex Luthor and lovely Lois Lane.

Now that you know you can run but you can't hide, let's get to work polishing your spelling.

No Windows or Heavy Lifting

In subsequent chapters, you'll learn the correct way to spell and form many words. For example, I'll teach you how to attach prefixes and suffixes, form contractions, and find silent letters. One of the keys to becoming a super speller, however, is not just memorizing a list of tricky words. Rather, your goal should be to:

- develop a system that will help you remember how to spell the words you already know; and
- increase your chances of correctly spelling many other words that you've yet to encounter.

The following guidelines can help you develop just such a strategy. Whatever your level of skill, you can benefit from the following time-tested spelling tricks. They're easy—and they work.

To get the greatest benefit from this section, read the guidelines through several times. Practice them with the spelling words I provide later in this chapter. Then use the guidelines as you work your way through this book.

SEE AND SAY. It's astonishing how many words are misspelled simply because the writer misses a sound or a syllable. Unstressed vowels and syllables are special villains. For example, *miniature* is often misspelled without that crucial second *i* because it is pronounced as *minature* rather than as *miniature*.

But let us not forget how often people insert an unnecessary vowel between two letters and so misspell the word. As a result of this mispronunciation, *jewelry* often becomes *jewelery*. Likewise, *remembrance* often masquerades as *rememberance*. Take a few moments to pronounce the following often mispronounced spelling demons. This will help you learn to spell them correctly:

accidentally
Arctic
diamond
eighth
lightning
original
recognize
symptom
veterinarian
umbrella

> "MY SPELLING IS WOBBLY. IT'S GOOD SPELLING BUT IT WOBBLES, AND LETTERS GET IN THE WRONG PLACES" (A. A. MILNE, AUTHOR OF **WINNIE THE POOH**).

There's more on this in Chapter 8, *Loose Lips Sink Ships*.

CLASSIFY ERRORS. Why not specialize? Figure out what words pose the most trouble for you and concentrate on those errors. For example, if you have a problem with words that contain *ie*, study the *ie* rule and concentrate on the words that follow the rules and the major exceptions.

BREAK DOWN WORDS INTO SMALLER PARTS. For example, to spell *bookkeeper*, break the word down to its two parts: *book* and *keeper*. Then you won't forget there's a double *k* in the middle of the word.

PUZZLE ME THIS. There are many different kinds of word puzzles and games to choose from, including crosswords, acrostics, Scrabble®, and Boggle®. Each type of word puzzle or game gives you practice spelling. As a bonus, doing puzzles also teaches you vocabulary. So what if it includes some useless words? You want everything?

USE PRINT DICTIONARIES. I know, I know, looking up a word is a pain. So is exercise, but they both work. Using a dictionary will help you remember a word's spelling and its exact meaning.

Actually, dictionaries give us a lot more than a list of words and their meanings. A good dictionary can be as useful as a good doctor, only a whole lot cheaper. There are two main kinds of dictionaries: *abridged* and *unabridged*.

An *unabridged* dictionary is complete. The *Oxford English Dictionary* (OED) is the standard unabridged dictionary. It contains more than 500,000 entries. Don't rush right out to buy one to stash in your briefcase, however; it attempts to record the birth and history of every printed word in the language since about A.D. 1000 to the current date of publication. The OED now contains about 60 million words in 20 volumes.

An *abridged* dictionary is shortened. It is fine for everyday purposes, like looking up words and silencing howling cats. But you'll want the unabridged dictionary if you're interested in knowing everything there is to know about a word.

Unless you're a dictionary collector, replace your dictionary every ten years, if not sooner.

To make your shopping trip easier, listed below are five of the standard abridged dictionaries you may wish to consider. Compare them to see which one best suits your needs. You will find that several dictionaries claim the name Webster's, after the early American lexicographer, Noah Webster. Since his name is in the public domain and not copyrighted, it's fair game for one and all.

Webster's New World Dictionary of the American Language
Webster's New Collegiate Dictionary (latest edition)
The American Heritage Dictionary
The Concise Oxford Dictionary of Current English
The Random House College Dictionary

If you find that your job or lifestyle requires you to know how to spell regional and foreign terms, you may wish to consult one of the following specialized dictionaries:

> A GOOD DICTIONARY WILL INCLUDE SPELLING VARIATIONS, ESPECIALLY BRITISH VERSUS AMERICAN SPELLING. TODAY'S DICTIONARIES ARE MORE ACCEPTING OF VARIANT SPELLINGS. SO WHEN IN DOUBT, USE YOUR BEST JUDGMENT.

Dictionary of American Regional English
Dictionary of Foreign Phrases and Abbreviations
Dictionary of Foreign Terms
Harper Dictionary of Foreign Terms

USE COMPUTER SPELL CHECKERS. Computer *spell check* programs call attention to any words that they cannot match to their own dictionaries. As a result, the programs are a great help in spotting errors. Spell check programs are included with nearly all word-processing packages.

But like all good things, these spell check programs have their limits. They are useless with homonyms, for example. If you intended to type "there" but instead wrote "they're," the spell checker will not pick this up as an error because you spelled "they're" correctly. Therefore, you must still proofread your documents carefully to make sure that you used the words you intended to use. The following poem illustrates my point:

Who wood have guest
The Spell Chequer would super seed
The assent of the editor
Who was once a mane figure?
Once, awl sought his council;
Now nun prophet from him.
How suite the job was;
It was all sew fine . . .
Never once was he board
As he edited each claws,
Going strait to his deer work
Where he in cysts on clarity.
Now he's holy unacceptable,
Useless and knot kneaded . . .
This is know miner issue,
For he cannot urn a wage.
Two this he takes a fence,
Butt nose naught watt too due.
He's wade each option
Of jobs he mite dew,
But nothing peaks his interest

> PRINT DICTIONARIES DON'T RUN OUT OF BATTERIES; HANDHELD COMPUTERIZED DICTIONARIES ARE LIGHT AND EASY TO CARRY. IT'S YOUR CALL. JUST BE SURE TO USE A DICTIONARY WHEN YOU CAN.

Like making pros clear.
Sum will see him silly
For being sew upset,
But doesn't good righting
Go beyond the write spelling?

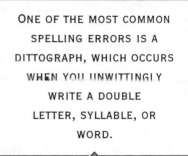

ONE OF THE MOST COMMON
SPELLING ERRORS IS A
DITTOGRAPH, WHICH OCCURS
WHEN YOU UNWITTINGLY
WRITE A DOUBLE
LETTER, SYLLABLE, OR
WORD.

You can customize your own on-screen dictionary by adding words to your spell checker. (I add all the proper nouns I regularly use, for example.) Beefing up your computerized spell checker isn't enough to make you a super speller—especially since most people can't whip out that laptop at a moment's notice.

SEVENTH INNING STRETCH

Take a stretch by completing this easy quiz. In each of the following groups of words, only one word is spelled correctly. In each group, select the correctly spelled word and write it in the space provided.

1. writting.........lightning.........inedable.........inocuous

2. lovabble.........veterinarian.........its'.........laborotory

3. accidentally.........summery.........bycycle.........laible

4. tradgey.........limosine.........recognize.........mispell

5. conceeding.........original.........ninty.........murmer

6. ilegal.........symptom.........on sequitior.........pagent

7. cival.........Arctic.........ocassion.........occurrennce

8. pittiful.........opthalmalogy.........umbrella.........partime

9. innocullate.........eighth.........pallette.........parimutel

10. intersede.........diamond.........passtime.........parlament

TRY AIR WRITING. No, it's not a New Age crystal thing; it's what Miss Nelson taught you in the fourth grade. To check the spelling of a word or to learn the spelling of an unfamiliar word, try writing it in the air.

GUESS AND CHECK. It's a free country; you're allowed to guess. To check the spelling of a word, make a guess. Write it down and see how it looks. You'll be

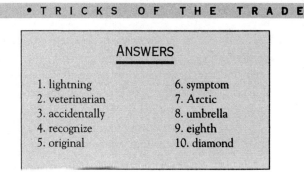

able to see if you're right or wrong and also probably to see *where* you went wrong: omitted letter, double letter, wrong letter. You can even try two or three different ways to write the word. Best case scenario: only one way will be right.

You might ask, "Why not just look the word up in the dictionary and be done with it?" No doubt that looking a word up in the dictionary is the best way to check its spelling, but let's get real. Everyone knows that saving for a rainy day and looking both ways before crossing the street are also solid pieces of advice—but how often do we follow those?

Besides, you might not always have a dictionary handy. For example, what happens if you're in a meeting and the boss asks you to write a brief memo? You're really going to take out a dictionary to check the spelling of a word? Why not just wear a sign that reads, "I can't spell so maybe I shouldn't have this job"?

USE WORD CARDS. Those flash cards you used in elementary school still work quite nicely with spelling. Try this three-step plan:

1. As you read through the following chapters, write each difficult spelling word on a three-by-five index card, one word per card.
2. Study the cards every chance you get.
3. Take them with you on the bus, train, and plane; hide them in your lap and sneak a peek during dull meetings.

VISUALIZE. In many cases, a little thinking about how the word is spelled can help you get it right. This process is called "visualization." It can help you remember the word and spell it correctly in the future. To make it work for you, follow these three easy steps:

1. Think about how the word is spelled.
2. Get a clear mental picture of the word.
3. Go over each letter in your mind.

USE MNEMONICS. *Mnemonics* are memory tricks that help you remember everything from the order of the planets to your grocery list. Mnemonics are especially useful for remembering how to spell tricky words. For example, to remember how to spell *principal*, look at the last three letters: the princi**pal** is your **pal**. *Principle*, in contrast, ends in *le*, like ru*le* (which is what *principle* means).

Here are some other well-known spelling mnemonics:

Word	Mnemonic
stationary	stationary means standing still
stationery	stationery is for letters
piece	a piece of the pie
believe	Don't believe that lie!
beginning	the beginning of the inning
friend	a friend to the end
there	There, here, where, all refer to a place
existence	Existence is often tense
accept	Accept this package
except	To except is to exclude
definite	definite is final!
capitol	Senators toil in the Capitol Building

You can even remember how to spell the word *mnemonic* with a memory trick. Mnemonic is a tricky spelling word because the initial *m* is silent. But if you know that a *m*nemonic is a *m*emory device, you've made it to third base. Now, just remember that both words begin with *m* and you've got a home run.

One of the most effective memory tricks is to first learn the correct pronunciation of a word and then mispronounce the word to highlight the correct spelling. I do this with *conscience* (often confused with *conscious*) by mentally saying it as CON-SCIENCE. Try it with *noticeable*, too. Pronounce the word NOTICE-EEEE-ABLE, so you don't forget that first *e*.

> SOMEONE ASKED
> A FOOL, "IS
> **KABOB** WITH AN
> **O** OR AN **A**?"
> "WITH MEAT,"
> HE ANSWERED.

Create your own mnemonics to conquer spelling demons. No matter how silly these memory tricks may seem, if they work for you, go with them.

COFFEE BREAK

You don't need all that caffeine. Instead, why not take this simple test? Write each of the following words correctly on the line provided. As you work, note which techniques you used to help you correct the words.

No-no	Yes-yes
1 Phillippines	
2. seperate	
3. anacdote	
4. envalope	
5. sewege	
6. phenmenon	
7. annoint	
8. twefth	
9. scalple	
10. perrenial	

TAKE ME TO YOUR RULER. Like indulgent parents, the English language is notorious for setting rules and breaking them. Take the *i* before *e* except after *c* rule, for instance. Even though *grief*, *piece*, *chief*, and *achieve* fit the rule, what are we to do with *either*, *height*, *foreigner*, and *weird*? (More on this in Chapter 4, "Follow the Rules.") Tempting though this inconsistency seems, don't use it as an excuse to ignore spelling rules.

LEARN WORD FAMILIES. Word families are, in effect, spelling patterns. People who learn many common word families also learn something more important: how to look carefully at the spelling pattern of a new word and search through the words they already know for words with the same spelling pattern. More on this later.

MAKE SURE YOU HAVE THE RIGHT WORD. Many words are confused with their first cousins. Sometimes these

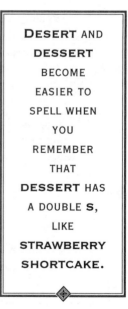

DESERT AND **DESSERT** BECOME EASIER TO SPELL WHEN YOU REMEMBER THAT **DESSERT** HAS A DOUBLE **S**, LIKE **STRAWBERRY SHORTCAKE.**

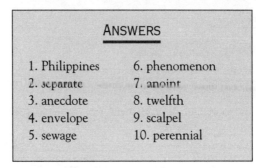

ANSWERS

1. Philippines   6. phenomenon
2. separate   7. anoint
3. anecdote   8. twelfth
4. envelope   9. scalpel
5. sewage   10. perennial

are genuine homonyms and homophones, such as *their*, *there*, and *they're* or *allot* and *a lot*. Other times, they are first cousins, such as *antidote* and *anecdote*. You don't have to worry about labeling the words. (Are these homophones or what?) Just make sure you have the word you want—before you even worry about spelling it.

MEMORIZE THE TRICKY ONES. Spelling, like a relationship, is especially vulnerable to mind games. Words can play amazing tricks on you. It may seem that a word should be spelled one way, but in fact, it is spelled in a completely different way. Take the word *experiential*, for example. Since *experiential* comes from *experience*, you would think it should be spelled with a *c*, like this: *experiencial*. Not so.

So after you've used all the strategies you learned here, such as pronouncing the word, creating memory devices, and relying on rules, recognize that there are some words that just don't play fair. There are many reasons for this, which I discuss in Chapter 9. The moral of the story: There are some words whose spelling you just have to memorize.

ONE MORE TIME. Let's pull it together with a final itty-bitty little quiz. Take a few minutes to find and circle the correctly spelled word in each group. Think about which techniques you used.

THEN THERE WAS THE BOY WHO SAID, "I CAN SPELL **BANANA** ALL RIGHT, ONLY I DON'T KNOW WHERE TO STOP."

1. achieve.........wierd..........profesy

2. acknowledgeable.........pronounciation.........vacilate

3. greif.........acommodate.........saccharin

4. ryhme.........tortuous.........vegatable

5. chief.........apraise.........sutle

6. baptizm.........rythm.........waiver

7. foriegner.........samon.........sandwich

8. peice.........either.........unnecesary

9. biege.........brethren.........vauge

10. proscribe.........hieght.........sucesful

ANSWERS

1. achieve	6. waiver
2. acknowledgeable	7. sandwich
3. saccharin	8. either
4. tortuous	9. brethren
5. chief	10. proscribe

IF ENGLISH IS NOT YOUR BIRTH LANGUAGE, YOU MIGHT HAVE A HARD TIME DIFFERENTIATING BETWEEN SHORT **A** AND SHORT **E**. PRACTICE WITH THESE WORD PAIRS: **DAN/DEN, PAT/PET, SAT/SET, MAT/MET**. UNDERLINE THE VOWELS IN EACH PAIR.

CHAPTER 2

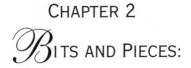

BITS AND PIECES:

PREFIXES AND SUFFIXES

YOU MUST REMEMBER THIS
A *prefix* is a group of letters put at the beginning of a word to change its meaning; a *suffix* does the same at the rear end.

ALL THE RIGHT MOVES
Spelling words with prefixes is a snap: just remember not to add or subtract any letters when you attach a prefix. Now, suffixes—they're a whole 'nother kettle of fish.

Prefixes are word parts you add to the beginning of a word to change its meaning; suffixes are word parts you add to the end of a word to change its meaning. Since many useful words are created by adding prefixes and suffixes to root words, you can save a lot of time wondering, "Did I spell this one correctly?" by knowing how to add prefixes and suffixes. Let's take a look at the guidelines.

FRONT-END COLLISION: ATTACHING PREFIXES

The rule here is simple: don't add or omit a letter when you attach a prefix. Keep all the letters—every one of them. Here are some examples:

Prefix		Root Word		New Word
a-	+	sexual	=	asexual
be-	+	moan	=	bemoan
circum-	+	scribe	=	circumscribe

Prefix		Root Word		New Word
dis-	+	satisfied	=	dissatisfied
im-	+	part	=	impart
inter-	+	related	=	interrelated
mis-	+	spell	=	misspell
over-	+	come	=	overcome
para-	+	phrase	=	paraphrase
re-	+	turn	=	return
un-	+	acceptable	=	unacceptable

MIX 'N' MATCH

Complete the following chart by creating new words as indicated.

Prefix		Root Word		New Word
1. circum-	+	locution	=	
2. co-	+	write	=	
3. dis-	+	agree	=	
4. ex-	+	change	=	
5. in-	+	scribe	=	
6. circum-	+	navigate	=	
7. re-	+	cover	=	
8. a-	+	typical	=	
9. epi-	+	graph	=	
10. para-	+	legal	=	

REAR-END COLLISION: ATTACHING SUFFIXES

In general, keep all the letters when you add a suffix . . . unless the word ends in a y or a silent e. We'll talk about *them* later. The following chart and guidelines show you how to master the suffix situation:

Word		Suffix		New Word
accident	+	-al	=	accidental
drunken	+	-ness	=	drunkenness

ANSWERS

1. circumlocution	6. circumnavigate
2. cowrite	7. recover
3. disagree	8. atypical
4. exchange	9. epigraph
5. inscribe	10. paralegal

---

foresee	+	-able	=	foreseeable
ski	+	-ing	=	skiing

1. If the letter before the final y is a consonant, change the y to i and add the suffix. Study these examples:

Word		**Suffix**		**New Word**
greedy	+	-ly	=	greedily
hurry	+	-ed	=	hurried
pony	+	-es	=	ponies
query	+	-es	=	queries

Hurry doesn't always follow the rule: *hurry* + *ing* = *hurrying.* Here are some other exceptions:

> KNOWING THE
> ROOT OF A
> WORD WILL
> HELP YOU
> CORRECTLY ADD
> PREFIXES AND
> SUFFIXES.

babyish	ladylike
dryly	dryness
shyly	shyness
spryness	miscellaneous

2. If the letter before the final y is a vowel, do not change the y before attaching a suffix.

Word		**Suffix**		**New Word**
destroy	+	-ed	=	destroyed
play	+	-ing	=	playing

Here are some exceptions:

laid	said
mislaid	underpaid
paid	unsaid

3. If the word begins with a vowel or a vowel sound, drop the silent *e*. Here are some examples:

Word		Suffix		New Word
ache	+	-ing	=	aching
argue	+	-ing	=	arguing
enclose	+	-sure	=	enclosure
illustrate	+	-ive	=	illustrative
use	+	-age	=	usage

4. When the word ends in *ce* or *ge*, keep the *e* if the suffix begins with *a* or *o*, as in these examples: *noticeable*, *manageable*, *advantageous*. Here are some exceptions:

Word		Suffix		New Word
acre	+	-age	=	acreage
canoe	+	-ing	=	canoeing
hoe	+	-ing	=	hoeing
mile	+	-age	=	mileage
singe	+	-ing	=	singeing

This also applies to -y suffixes:

Word		Suffix		New Word
mange	+	-y	=	mangy
sponge	+	-y	=	spongy
stone	+	-y	=	stony
wire	+	-y	=	wiry

Of course there are some exceptions, such as *cagey* and *homey*.

5. If the suffix begins with a consonant, keep the silent *e*. Here are some examples:

Word		Suffix		New Word
care	+	-ful	=	careful
excite	+	-ment	=	excitement
fierce	+	-ly	=	fiercely
sore	+	-ly	=	sorely

Naturally, there are some exceptions. Here are a few of the most annoying ones:

argument   awfully   ninth   truly   wholly

6. If the word ends in *ie*, drop the *e* and change the *i* to *y*. Check out these examples:

Word		Suffix		New Word
die	+	-ing	=	dying
lie	+	-ing	=	lying
tie	+	-ing	=	tying

END GAME

Take a break to assess your progress. Complete the following chart by adding each suffix to its root word. All's fair in love, war, and spelling, so feel free to look back at the rules you've already learned.

Word		Suffix		New Word
1. disparage	+	-ment	=	
2. argue	+	-ing	=	
3. comply	+	-ance	=	
4. imply	+	-ing	=	
5. blue	+	-ness	=	
6. lay	+	-ed	=	
7. care	+	-ful	=	
8. profuse	+	-ly	=	
9. tie	+	-ing	=	
10. vie	+	-ing	=	
11. dainty	+	-ness	=	
12. lie	+	-ing	=	
13. mile	+	-age	=	
14. bare	+	-ly	=	

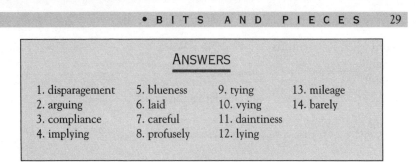

ANSWERS

1. disparagement	5. blueness	9. tying	13. mileage
2. arguing	6. laid	10. vying	14. barely
3. compliance	7. careful	11. daintiness	
4. implying	8. profusely	12. lying	

(You're in the home stretch—just a few more rules to go.)

7. Add *-ly* to change an adjective to an adverb. Here are some examples:

Adjective		Suffix		New Word
brave	+	*-ly*	=	bravely
calm	+	*-ly*	=	calmly

If the adjective ends in *-ic*, add *-al* before *-ly*.

Adjective		Al		Suffix		New Word
drastic	+	*-al*	+	*-ly*	=	drastically
scientific	+	*-al*	+	*-ly*	=	scientifically

If the adjective ends in *-ble*, change *-ble* to *-bly*.

Adjective		Suffix		New Word
able	+	*-ly*	=	ably
noble	+	*-ly*	=	nobly

8. In a one-syllable word, double the final consonant before adding a suffix beginning with a vowel.

Word		Suffix		New Word
big	+	*-est*	=	biggest
plan	+	*-er*	=	planner
stop	+	*-ed*	=	stopped

Don't double the final consonant if it comes after two vowels or another consonant. For example: *failed, stooped, warmer, lasting.* Also, don't double the final consonant if the accent shifts back to the first syllable, as in these examples:

Word		Suffix		New Word
conFER	+	-ence	=	CONference
preFER	+	-ence	=	PREFerence
reFER	+	-ence	=	REFerence

An exception is the word *excellent*. Here, exCel + *ence* = EXcellence.

9. In a word of two or more syllables, double the final consonant when it's in an accented syllable before a suffix beginning with a vowel. Here are some examples:

Word		Suffix		New Word
deFER	+	-ed	=	deferred
resubMIT	+	-ing	=	resubmitting

Don't double the final consonant if it comes after two vowels or another consonant. For example: *obtained, concealed, abducting, commendable*.

10. If a word ends in *-ic*, insert a *k* after the *c* before adding a suffix.

> THE LETTER COMBINATION **SH** CAN BE SPELLED FOURTEEN DIFFERENT WAYS. NO WONDER YOU BOUGHT THIS BOOK!

Word		Suffix		New Word
frolic	+	-ed	=	frolicked
mimic	+	-er	=	mimicker
traffic	+	-ing	=	trafficking

END RUN

Take a break to assess your progress. Complete the following chart by adding each suffix to its root word. Remember, it's okay to look back at the rules you've already learned.

Word		Suffix		New Word
1. quick	+	-ly	=	
2. noble	+	-ly	=	
3. tan	+	-er	=	

ANSWERS

1. quickly	6. systematically	11. reference
2. nobly	7. frolicking	12. smoothly
3. tanner	8. shellacker	13. deferred
4. excellence	9. mopped	14. digger
5. commendable	10. failed	15. artistically

4. excel	+	-ence	=	
5. commend	+	-able	=	
6. systematic	+	-ly	=	
7. frolic	+	-ing	=	
8. shellac	+	-er	=	
9. mop	+	-ed	=	
10. fail	+	-ed	=	
11. refer	+	-ence	=	
12. smooth	+	-ly	=	
13. defer	+	-ed	=	
14. dig	+	-er	=	
15. artistic	+	-ly	=	

11. Adding *-able* and *-ible:* After a complete word, the suffix is usually spelled *-able* rather than *-ible*. For instance:

> fixable   breakable
> workable   predictable

What's a language without exceptions? Here are some of the most often used (and most often misused ones): *discernible, dismissible, resistible, gullible, flexible.*

An adjective usually ends in *-ible* if you can trace it back to a noun ending in *-ion,* for example:

Noun	Adjective
accession	accessible
collection	collectible
digestion	digestible
expansion	extensible
repression	repressible
sensation	sensible

But there are many words that don't fit this rule, so this isn't the rule to have tattooed on your palm. Exceptions include *predictable*, *correctable*, *adaptable*.

A word ending in *e* preceded by a single consonant usually drops the *e* and takes *-able*:

comparable	desirable
measurable	writable

However, the word *sizable* has variant spellings. Both *sizable* and *sizeable* are acceptable.

When the word ends in *-ce* or *-ge* with a soft sound, keep the *e* before *-able*. This keeps the soft sound, as in *peaceable* and *changeable*. When the *-ce* or *-ge* are hard, drop the *e*, as in *implacable*, *practicable*, and *despicable*.

After the letter *i*, the suffix is always spelled *-able*. Here are some examples that drive spellers mad:

amiable	appreciable
enviable	insatiable
justifiable	sociable

When a root ends in *-miss* or *-ns*, the suffix is always *-ible*, as in these words:

admissible	comprehensible
dismissible	ostensible
permissible	transmissible

Here are two exceptions to this rule: *dispensable*, *indispensable*.

Since we have so many *-ables* and *-ibles*, you may wish to review this chart with the most common words that take one or the other of these suffixes:

Words with -able   Words with -ible

Words with -able	Words with -ible
acceptable	accessible
adaptable	admissible
amiable	audible
appreciable	collapsible
believable	contemptible
bendable	comprehensible
breakable	credible
changeable	digestible
charitable	dismissible
comparable	dispersible
correctable	eligible
debatable	feasible
desirable	flexible
despicable	forcible
enviable	gullible
excusable	indelible
favorable	inexhaustible
fixable	intelligible
formidable	invincible
implacable	legible
incurable	negligible
indefatigable	ostensible
insatiable	permissible
justifiable	repressible
manageable	resistible
measurable	sensible
memorable	tangible
peaceable	transmissible
practicable	visible
predictable	
preferable	
profitable	
reliable	
sizable, sizeable	
sociable	
workable	
writable	

THERE ARE MORE **-ABLE** WORDS THAN **-IBLE**, SO IF YOU'RE IN A PRESSURE SITUATION, GO WITH **-ABLE**.

ISH-KA-BIBALE?

Write the words formed by adding the suffix -able or -ible.

1. sens	9. us
2. memor	10. lov
3. work	11. access
4. gull	12. change
5. believ	13. collect
6. feas	14. manage
7. implac	15. elig
8. cred	

ANSWERS

1. sensible	6. feasible	11. accessible
2. memorable	7. implacable	12. changeable
3. workable	8. credible	13. collectible
4. gullible	9. usable	14. manageable
5. believable	10. lovable	15. eligible

12. What about the suffixes -ant/-ance and -ent/-ence? Unfortunately, there's no solid rule here, but I can give you some guidelines. In general, -ence words are more common than -ance words—except after the letters v and t. Here are some examples:

assistance   observance   pittance   relevance   reluctance

In addition, the suffix is usually -ence after a soft g or c, as in these spelling monsters:

diligence   intelligence   munificence   phosphorescence

The suffix is usually -ance if the g or c is hard. For instance:

extravagance   significance

The following lists summarize the most frequently misspelled -ant/-ance/-ancy and -ent/-ence/-ency words:

-ant/-ance/-ancy   **-ent/-ence/-ency**
aberrance   adherence

-ant/-ance/-ancy	-ent/-ence/-ency
abundance	adolescence
assistance	antecedent
attendance	coherence
cognizant	convalescence
compliance	correspondence
defiance	currency
extravagance	decadence
fragrance	despondent
hesitancy	diligence
ignorance	eloquence
inconstancy	eminence
lieutenant	fluency
nonchalance	frequency
observance	imminence
petulance	incompetence
pittance	intelligence
poignancy	munificence
relevance	negligence
reliance	opulence
reluctance	permanence
repentance	pertinence
resistance	phosphorescence
significance	potency
sufferance	recurrence
truancy	resplendent
vagrancy	urgency
vigilance	vehemence

-ANCE IN YOUR PANCE?

Complete each word by filling in *-ance/-ant* or *-ence/-ent*.

1. aberr

2. despond

3. relev

4. opul

5. suffer

6. petul

7. anteced

8. resplend

9. lieuten

10. cogniz

ANSWERS

1. aberrance	4. opulence	7. antecedent
2. despondent	5. sufferance	8. resplendent
3. relevant	6. petulance	9. lieutenant
		10. cognizant

---

13. Use *-ify* or *-efy*? In most cases, the suffix will be spelled *-ify* rather than *-efy*. Exceptions include *rarefy*, *liquefy*, and *putrefy*.

14. Use *-ise* or *-ize*? After the letter *v*, the suffix is always *-ise*, never *-ize*. Here are some examples: *supervise*, *revise*, *advise*.

15. Use *-er* or *-or*? Verbs ending in *-ate* usually become nouns ending in *-or* rather than *-er*. Here are some examples:

Verb	Noun
create	creator
demonstrate	demonstrator
indicate	indicator
liberate	liberator

> THERE ARE SIX WORDS IN ENGLISH WITH THE LETTER COMBINATION UU: MUUMUU, VACUUM, CONTINUUM, RESIDUUM, DUUMVIRATE, AND DUUMVIR.

One exception? (You knew there just had to be at least one, didn't you?) It's *debate/debater*. Aside from this rule, there's no easy way to tell whether a noun ends in *-or* rather than *-er*. Here are some words to study:

Using *-er*	Using *-or*
consumer	aggressor
coroner	ambassador

defender
dissenter
interpreter
invader
laborer
organizer
philosopher
pretender
purchaser
subscriber
supporter
sympathizer

censor
contributor
creditor
debtor
governor
monitor
possessor
professor
prosecutor
tailor
traitor
vendor

END OF THE LINE

Fill in this chart by adding each suffix to its root word. It's still okay to look back at the rules you've already learned.

Word		Suffix		New Word
1. liquid	+	-fy	=	
2. bet	+	-or	=	
3. consume	+	-er	=	
4. contribute	+	-or	=	
5. indicate	+	-or	=	
6. beauty	+	-fy	=	
7. sympathize	+	-er	=	
8. debate	+	-or	=	
9. liberate	+	-or	=	
10. stupe	+	-fy	=	

ANSWERS

1. liquefy	4. contributor	7. sympathizer	10. stupefy
2. bettor	5. indicator	8. debater	
3. consumer	6. beautify	9. liberator	

CHAPTER 3

$\mathcal{Q}$UICK CHANGE ARTISTS:

CONTRACTIONS, POSSESSIVES,

AND PLURALS

YOU MUST REMEMBER THIS

Contractions, possessives, and plurals present intriguing challenges. There are rules . . . but there are also exceptions.

ALL THE RIGHT MOVES

In general, the apostrophe goes where the letter or letters have been omitted in a contraction.

When English was young, spelling was, well, *individualistic*. Even William Shakespeare couldn't figure out a standard way to spell his own name: several variations on "Shakespeare" appear in his plays and in his last will and testament—even on his tombstone. I can load you down with examples that prove the idiosyncrasies of early English spelling, but you get the general idea.

Fortunately for all of us, by the time Samuel Johnson published his landmark *Dictionary of the English Language* in 1755, spelling was fairly standardized. Yet Johnson's primary basis for the spellings he used in his dictionary was word history (*etymology*), not phonetic aptness or simplicity. *Uh oh.*

In 1828, American Noah Webster weighed in with his soon-to-be famous *American Dictionary of the English Language* and his *American Spelling Book*. The latter became the touchstone for good spelling. It underwent several hundred revisions and sold more than 60 million copies.

TRADITIONALLY, CONTRACTIONS ARE NOT USED IN FORMAL WRITING, SUCH AS REPORTS AND LETTERS. THAT'S ONE WAY OF GETTING OUT OF HAVING TO SPELL THEM!

When standardized spelling was finally achieved, it was often unphonetic and did not reflect what people were actually saying. Nonetheless, by the 1900s, the dictionary had become an institution, like the Smithsonian, Harvard, and Bob Hope. From then on, people like you and me sought "correctness" in speech and language. It became one of the signs of an educated, intelligent person. In this chapter, you'll learn how to deal with some of the most common and thorniest spelling situations—those involving contractions, possessives, and plurals.

CONTRACTIONS

Creating contractions is another useful skill, right up there with knowing how to work an ATM, execute a three-point turn, and rappel down a cliff. Fortunately, it's much easier to learn how to form contractions.

The basic rule for forming a contraction is a snap. When combining two words, just insert an apostrophe in the space where the letter or letters have been omitted. Here are some examples:

Word 1		Word 2		Contraction
can	+	not	=	can't
could	+	not	=	couldn't
does	+	not	=	doesn't
has	+	not	=	hasn't
he	+	is	=	he's
he	+	will	=	he'll
I	+	am	=	I'm
I	+	have	=	I've
it	+	is	=	it's
it	+	will	=	it'll
let	+	us	=	let's
must	+	not	=	mustn't
she	+	would	=	she'd
she	+	will	=	she'll
there	+	is	=	there's
they	+	are	=	they're
they	+	will	=	they'll
was	+	not	=	wasn't
we	+	are	=	we're
we	+	have	=	we've
we	+	would	=	we'd

Word 1		Word 2		Contraction
we	+	will	=	we'll
were	+	not	=	weren't
who	+	is	=	who's
would	+	not	=	wouldn't
you	+	are	=	you're
you	+	have	=	you've

Don't confuse *contractions* with *possessive pronouns*. Study this chart to compare the two:

Contraction	Possessive Pronoun
it's (it is)	its
they're (they are)	their
who's (who is)	whose
you're (you are)	your

> HERE'S A KEY
> EXCEPTION: **WILL +
> NOT = WON'T**
> (NOT **WILLN'T**)

SQUEEZE PLAY

Make each of the underlined phrases into a contraction.

1. When you <u>do not</u> know what to do, walk fast and look worried.

_____

2. People who go to conferences are the ones who <u>should not.</u>

_____

3. If it <u>were not</u> for the last minute, nothing would get done.

_____

4. <u>Do not</u> be irreplaceable; if you <u>can not</u> be replaced, you <u>can not</u> be promoted.

_____

5. It <u>does not</u> matter what you do, it only matters what you say <u>you have</u> done and what <u>you are</u> going to do.

_____

6. <u>It is</u> more fun to color outside the lines.

_____

7. Even if <u>you have</u> been fishing for three hours and you <u>have not</u> gotten anything except poison ivy and a sunburn, <u>you are</u> still better off than the worm.

_____

8. According to Albert Einstein, "Only two things are infinite, the universe and human stupidity, and <u>I am</u> not sure about the former."

9. The lightbulbs in the New York subway system screw in clockwise and screw out counter-clockwise—the reverse of traditional lightbulbs. This is so that people who steal them <u>can not</u> use them.

10. A solar flare has hit earth but <u>is not</u> expected to disrupt television transmissions, telephone lines, or computer networks. These tasks still fall, respectively, to infomercials, nagging parents, and your internet provider.

ANSWERS

1. don't
2. shouldn't
3. weren't
4. Don't, can't, can't
5. doesn't, you've, you're

6. it's
7. you've, haven't, you're
8. I'm
9. can't
10. isn't

TURNABOUT IS FAIR PLAY

This time, change the contraction into the two words it replaced. Here is an example:

Hilton Hotels plans to build Paris in Las Vegas, with an Eiffel Tower replica, and a 3,000-room hotel and casino. <u>It's</u> (it is) very authentic. The only act is Jerry Lewis, the dealers ignore you, and there is no soap.

1. *The New York Times* says 10 percent of the NFL's players are addicted to painkillers. <u>It's</u> peer pressure. Many players feel that if you <u>can't</u> wrap your car around a tree and walk away, you <u>don't</u> belong in the game.

---

2. The IRS: <u>We've</u> got what it takes to get what <u>you've</u> got.

---

3. "<u>I've</u> had a wonderful evening, but this <u>wasn't</u> it," was one of Groucho Marx's standard lines.

4. So I went to my doctor, and he said, "You're sick." I said, "I want a second opinion." He said, "<u>You're</u> ugly, too."

5. So I went to my doctor, and I said, "<u>Don't</u> tell me I'm overweight." He said, "Okay, <u>you're</u> four inches too short."

6. So after the operation, I went to my doctor and I said, "Will I ever be able to play the piano again?" He said, "Certainly." I said, "<u>That's</u> funny. I <u>couldn't</u> play it before."

ANSWERS

1. it is, can not, do not
2. we have, you have
3. I have, was not
4. you are, you are
5. do not, you are
6. that is, could not

TWO'S COMPANY, THREE'S A CROWD: PLURALS

Singular or *plural* refers to the number of a given noun, or how many are being signified. *Singular* indicates "one"; *plural* indicates "more then one."

Plural nouns name more than one person, place, or thing. There are regular plurals and irregular ones. The regular plurals rarely result in spelling errors, but those darned irregular plurals often cause trouble. Keep regular and irregular plurals straight and you'll eliminate a lot of spelling errors.

Follow these guidelines to form the plural of nouns:

1. Most regular plurals are formed by adding *s* to the end of the word.

Singular	Plural
arrow	arrows
bird	birds
dog	dogs

duck	ducks
hat	hats
pencil	pencils

2. Add -es if the noun ends in s, sh, ch, or x.

> IF ENGLISH IS NOT YOUR FIRST LANGUAGE, YOU MIGHT FIND THE ADDITION OF AN **-S** TO THE THIRD PERSON SINGULAR VERB PROBLEMATIC. PAY SPECIAL ATTENTION TO THIS WHEN YOU SPELL THESE VERBS.

Singular	Plural
belch	belches
box	boxes
class	classes
dish	dishes
inch	inches
Jones	Joneses
roach	roaches
sex	sexes
squelch	squelches
stress	stresses
tax	taxes

3. If the noun ends in -y preceded by a consonant, change the -y to -i and add -es. This is an irregular plural.

Singular	Plural
activity	activities
blueberry	blueberries
city	cities
cry	cries
lady	ladies

4. If the noun ends in -y preceded by a vowel, add -s. This is a regular plural.

Singular	Plural
attorney	attorneys
boy	boys
essay	essays
honey	honeys
journey	journeys
monkey	monkeys
survey	surveys
ray	rays

The exception? Words that end in *-quy*, as in soliloquy, which becomes soliloquies.

5. Words that end in *-ly* keep the y when they become plural.
For example:

Singular	Plural
bialy	bialys
fly	flys

Exceptions include *dollies, lilies*.

6. If the noun ends in *o* preceded by a *vowel*, add *-s*.

Singular	Plural
cameo	cameos
folio	folios
patio	patios
radio	radios
ratio	ratios
studio	studios

7. If the noun ends in *o* preceded by a consonant, the noun can take *-es*, *-s*, or either *-s* or *-es*.

	Singular	Plural
takes -es	echo	echoes
	hero	heroes
	potato	potatoes
	tomato	tomatoes
	veto	vetoes
takes -s	alto	altos
	dynamo	dynamos
	piano	pianos
	silo	silos
	solo	solos
	soprano	sopranos
either -es or -s	buffalo	buffalos, buffaloes
	cargo	cargos, cargoes
	domino	dominos, dominoes
	motto	mottos, mottoes
	tornado	tornados, tornadoes
	zero	zeros, zeroes

TOO MUCH OF A GOOD THING?

Before I overwhelm you with rules, take a break to make each of the following singular words plural. Write each answer in the space provided.

Singular	Plural
1. roach	
2. alto	
3. cameo	
4. lily	
5. sex	
6. cry	
7. potato	
8. kitten	
9. silo	
10. fez	

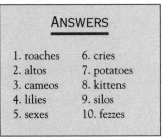

ANSWERS

1. roaches	6. cries
2. altos	7. potatoes
3. cameos	8. kittens
4. lilies	9. silos
5. sexes	10. fezzes

Back to the salt mines! Here are a few more guidelines for forming plurals:

8. Add -s to most nouns ending in *f*. However, the *f* endings are so irregular as to be nearly random. If you have any doubts at all, consult a dictionary.

Singular	Plural
belief	beliefs
brief	briefs
chief	chiefs
proof	proofs
sheriff	sheriffs
staff	staffs

In some cases, change the *f* or *fe* to *v* and add *-es:*

Singular	Plural
half	halves
knife	knives
leaf	leaves
life	lives
self	selves
thief	thieves
wife	wives
wolf	wolves

This rule doesn't hold for names. In that case, just add an *-s*: "Mr. and Ms. Wolf" becomes "The Wolfs."

9. Words that end in *-ey, -ay,* or *-oy* do not have *-ies* plurals.

Singular	Plural
abbey	abbeys
jitney	jitneys
valley	valleys
clay	clays
tray	trays
ploy	ploys

10. In compound words, make the main word plural.

Singular	Plural
mother-in-law	mothers-in-law
passerby	passersby
sister-in-law	sisters-in-law

There are two exceptions. The first is that if there is no noun in the compound word, add an *-s* to the end of the word, as follows:

Singular	Plural
mix-up	mix-ups
takeoff	takeoffs

The second is that if the compound word ends in *-ful*, add an *-s* to the end of the word, as follows:

Singular	Plural
cupful	cupfuls

But there are variant spellings.

11. Some nouns change their spelling when they become plural.

Singular	Plural
child	children
foot	feet
goose	geese
louse	lice
man	men
mouse	mice
ox	oxen
tooth	teeth
woman	women

12. Some nouns have the same form whether they are singular or plural.

Singular	Plural
deer	deer
moose	moose
Portuguese	Portuguese
series	series
sheep	sheep
species	species
swine	swine

13. The only plurals formed with apostrophes are the plurals of numbers, letters, and words highlighted as words. Here are some examples:

How many 3's make 9?
Be sure to mind your *p*'s and *q*'s.
How many s's are in "Mississippi"?
There were too many *but*'s in the speech.

14. Some words form plurals in other ways, which are often determined by the laws of their language of origin. Here are some examples:

Singular	Plural
alumna	alumnae
alumnus	alumni
analysis	analyses
axis	axes
bacterium	bacteria
basis	bases
crisis	crises
criterion	criteria
hypothesis	hypotheses
index	indexes, indices
memorandum	memorandums, memoranda
parenthesis	parentheses
phenomenon	phenomena
stimulus	stimuli
thesis	theses

> THE ONLY WORD THAT CONSISTS OF TWO LETTERS, EACH USED THREE TIMES, IS THE WORD **DEEDED**.

COMBO PLATTER

Write the plural of the following words:

Singular	Plural
1. spoonful	
2. sheriff	
3. Vietnamese	
4. chief	
5. moose	
6. axis	
7. wolf	
8. criterion	
9. stimulus	
10. basis	
11. index	

12. Lebanese

13. parenthesis

14. louse

15. bacterium

ANSWERS

1. spoonfuls	6. axes	11. indexes, indices
2. sheriffs	7. wolves	12. Lebanese
3. Vietnamese	8. criteria	13. parentheses
4. chiefs	9. stimuli	14. lice
5. moose	10. bases	15. bacteria

FROM THE FRYING PAN INTO THE FIRE?

Most plurals are a pretty straightforward affair, but every now and again we get some that are truly wicked. See how many of these spelling demons you can make plural—correctly. (Since all's fair in love, war, and plurals, feel free to consult a dictionary as you work.)

Singular	Plural
1. kielbasa	
2. coccyx	
3. nexus	
4. auto-da-fé	
5. kohlrabi	
6. pince-nez	
7. court-martial	
8. mot juste	
9. chassis	
10. heir apparent	

ANSWERS

(if you're still conscious after *that* experience)

1. kielbasas,   3. nexus, nexuses   7. courts-martial, court-martials
   kielbasy   4. autos-da-fé   8. mots justes
2. coccyxes,   5. kohlrabies   9. chassis, chassises
   coccyges   6. pince-nez (no change) 10. heirs apparent

IT'S MINE! I SAW IT FIRST! POSSESSION

Possession shows ownership. Follow these rules to create possessive nouns.

1. With singular nouns, add an apostrophe and an *-s*.

Not possessive	**Possessive**
girl	girl's manuscript
James	James's job
student	student's ideas

2. With plural nouns ending in *-s*, add an apostrophe after the *-s*.

Not possessive	**Possessive**
girls	girls' manuscripts
players	players' awards
workers	workers' ideas

> REMEMBER THAT POSSESSIVE PRONOUNS DO NOT REQUIRE AN APOSTROPHE. THE POSSESSIVE PRONOUNS ARE: **YOURS, HERS, ITS, OURS, THEIRS,** AND **WHOSE**. EXAMPLE: THE REPORT WAS **HERS**.

3. With plural nouns not ending in *-s*, add an apostrophe and an *-s*.

Not possessive	Possessive
men	men's belts
mice	mice's tails
sheep	sheep's bleats
women	women's books

4. To form the possessive of a business name, joint owner, or compound noun, put an apostrophe and *-s* after the last word.

Not possessive	Possessive
Bikel and Bikel	Bikel and Bikel's cases
Gilbert and Sullivan	Gilbert and Sullivan's operas
sister-in-law	sister-in-law's bracelet

IN MANY LANGUAGES OTHER THAN ENGLISH, THE OBJECT POSSESSED IS NAMED FIRST, FOLLOWED BY THE PERSON OR THING THAT POSSESSES IT. FOR EXAMPLE: "THIS IS THE OFFICE OF SPENCER." THE WAY POSSESSIVES ARE FORMED IN ENGLISH OFTEN POSES PROBLEMS FOR NON-NATIVE SPEAKERS.

SAVING SPACE

Reduce each of the following sentences to fewer words by using the possessive form. Here's an example:

Original:
The comedy routine of the Three Stooges isn't funny to me.

Revised:
The Three Stooges' comedy routine isn't funny to me.

1. The original name of Mel Brooks was Melvin Kaminsky.

_____

_____

2. The quack of a duck doesn't echo, and no one knows why.

_____

_____

3. The placement of the eyes of a donkey in its head enables it to see all four feet at all times.

_____

_____

4. The original name of Mickey Mouse was Mortimer Mouse.

_____

_____

5. The real name of Hulk Hogan is Terry Bollea.

_____

_____

6. The milk of a camel does not curdle.

_____

_____

7. In *Fantasia* by Disney, the name of the Sorcerer is Yensid, which is "Disney" reversed.

_____

8. The height of the Eiffel Tower varies by as much as six inches, depending on the temperature.

_____

_____

9. The favorite hobby of my mother-in-law is playing cards on her computer.

_____

10. Keep the boss of your boss off the back of your boss.

_____

_____

Answers

1. Mel Brooks's name was originally Melvin Kaminsky.
2. A duck's quack doesn't echo, and no one knows why.
3. The placement of a donkey's eyes in its head enables it to see its four feet at all times.
4. Mickey Mouse's original name was Mortimer Mouse.
5. Hulk Hogan's real name is Terry Bollea.
6. Camel's milk does not curdle.
7. In Disney's *Fantasia*, the Sorcerer's name is Yensid, which is "Disney" reversed.
8. The Eiffel Tower's height varies by as much as six inches, depending on the temperature.
9. My mother-in-law's favorite hobby is playing cards on her computer.
10. Keep your boss's boss off your boss's back.

A CORE OF ABOUT 5,000 WORDS ACCOUNTS FOR ABOUT 95 PERCENT OF THE WORDS ADULTS USE IN THEIR EVERY-DAY WRITING. NOW, IF YOU CAN JUST FIGURE OUT WHICH 5,000 WORDS YOU NEED TO KNOW HOW TO SPELL . . .

CHAPTER 4

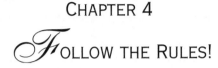OLLOW THE RULES!

SPELLING RULES, THAT IS

YOU MUST REMEMBER THIS
Spelling rules work! Try them for yourself.

ALL THE RIGHT MOVES
Memorize spelling rules and the common exceptions. Then apply the rules when you have to spell unfamiliar or tricky words.

Here are three rules to live by:

1. No one is listening until you make a mistake.
2. Experience is something you don't get until just after you need it.
3. They who hesitate are probably right.

Who can trust the rules of life? You really *can* go swimming right after you eat; winning sometimes *is* everything. Spelling, fortunately, has some valid rules. Here are some nifty ones that will serve you well.

1. **Use *i* before *e* except after *c*.** Remember this baby from the eighth grade (or were you too busy putting acne ointment on your nose to pay attention to something as mundane as spelling)? Anyway, here's the rule (and it even has a bouncy rhyme to it):

   I before *e* except after *c*
   or when it sounds like *a*
   as in *neighbor* and *weigh*.

Here are some words that fit the rule:

I before E	Except after C	Sounded as A
achieve	ceiling	beige
believe	conceit	eight
bier	conceive	feint
chief	deceit	freight
fiend	deceive	heir
fierce	perceive	neighbor
grief	receipt	reign
piece	receive	sleigh
relief		surveillance
relieve		weigh
shriek		weight
siege		veil
yield		vein

And here are some words that don't:

codeine	counterfeit	either
Fahrenheit	financier	foreign
glacier	height	leisure
neither	protein	seize
weird		

(Hey, is anything perfect? I never promised you a rose garden, only some nifty spelling rules.)

So how can you use this rule to its best advantage? Here are some suggestions:

•In most cases, when the c sounds like sh, the order of the letters is ie, not ei. Words that fit this rule include the following:

ancient	coefficient
conscientious	efficient
prescience	

•Think of *ie* and *ei* words that give you special trouble. Perhaps it's *financier*; maybe *foreign*. Make a special effort to memorize these rules. Use the rhyming rule to help you.

2. E, i, e, i (no o). Here are some additional guidelines to use when you spell words with *ei* and *ie* (Stick with me, now; there are a lot of useful English words with this letter combination):

•If the sound is a long *i*, the word is usually spelled with the *ei* combo, not *ie*. For example:

feisty   height
leitmotif   seismic
stein

Here are the common exceptions: *hierarchy*, *fiery*, and *hieroglyphic*. Notice that in each case, the *ie* combination is followed by an *r*.

•Words with a short vowel sound are usually spelled with *ie* rather than with *ei*. Here are some examples:

friend   handkerchief
mischief   patient
sieve

The exceptions (you knew I would say that, didn't you?) include the following words:

counterfeit   heifer
nonpareil   sovereign
surfeit

WHICH IS IT: IE OR EI?

Let's see, was it "i before e except after c" or "e before i except when there's pie in the sky"? Get that rule! I've set aside a nice bunch of *ie* and *ei* words for you to enjoy all at once. No need to thank me; just complete the following words by adding *ie* or *ei* as necessary.

1. w_____rd

2. cod_____ne

3. s_____ze

4. caff_____ne

5. forf_____t

6. dec_____ve

7. s_____ve

8. g_____sha

9. c_____ling

10. f_____nd

11. rec_____pt

12. conc_____ve

13. sk_____n

14. w_____ld

15. n_____ce

A LOOK THROUGH EARLY NEW ENGLAND LETTERS AND TOWN RECORDS REVEALS MORE THAN FIFTY SPELLINGS FOR **RECEIVE**. AMONG THE MOST CREATIVE WERE **RECEYVE, RESAIVED, RECUSED,** AND **RECEAUED**. FEEL BETTER?

ANSWERS

1. weird	6. deceive	11. receipt
2. codeine	7. sieve	12. conceive
3. seize	8. geisha	13. skein
4. caffeine	9. ceiling	14. wield
5. forfeit	10. fiend	15. niece

3. The *ceed/cede* rule. There are only three verbs in English that end in *ceed*: *succeed*, *proceed*, and *exceed*. All the other verbs with that sound end in *cede*. For example:

accede   cede
concede   intercede
precede   recede
secede

THERE IS ONLY ONE ENGLISH VERB THAT ENDS IN **-SEDE**: **SUPERSEDE.**

4. The *-ful* rule. Remember that the sound *full* at the end of a word is spelled with only one *l*. For example:

Root Word		Suffix		New Word
care	+	*-ful*	=	careful
grace	+	*-ful*	=	graceful
health	+	*-ful*	=	healthful
hope	+	*-ful*	=	hopeful

When the suffix is *-ful* plus *-ly*, there are two *l*'s. Here are some examples:

Root Word		Suffix		New Word
artful	+	*-ly*	=	artfully
baleful	+	*-ly*	=	balefully
mirthful	+	*-ly*	=	mirthfully
restful	+	*-ly*	=	restfully
thankful	+	*-ly*	=	thankfully
zestful	+	*-ly*	=	zestfully

5. Do I use *-ery* or *-ary*? Stumped when to use *-ery* or *-ary* at the end of a word? Try these guidelines. First of all, only six commonplace words end with *-ery* rather than *-ary*:

cemetery	confectionery
distillery	millinery
monastery	stationery (writing paper)

Therefore, if you have to guess, the big money's on *-ary* over *-ery*.

You Play, You Pay

Enough fun; it's time to strut your stuff. Spell each of the following words correctly. Then cite the rule that you used.

Spelling Word	Rule
1. superseed	
2. healthfull	
3. exced	
4. stationery (unmoving)	
5. balefuly	
6. confectionary	
7. interceede	
8. mirthfuly	
9. monastary	
10. preceede	

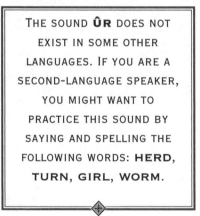

THE SOUND **ÛR** DOES NOT EXIST IN SOME OTHER LANGUAGES. IF YOU ARE A SECOND-LANGUAGE SPEAKER, YOU MIGHT WANT TO PRACTICE THIS SOUND BY SAYING AND SPELLING THE FOLLOWING WORDS: **HERD, TURN, GIRL, WORM.**

ANSWERS

Spelling Word	Rule
1. supersede	This is the only English verb that ends in *sede*.
2. healthful	The sound *full* at the end of a word is spelled with only one *l*.
3. exceed	There are only three verbs in English that end in *ceed* . . . and this is one of them.
4. stationary	Only six commonplace words end with *-ery* as opposed to *-ary* . . . and this is not one of them.
5. balefully	When the suffix is *-ful* plus *-ly*, there are two *l*'s.
6. confectionery	Only six commonplace words end with *-ery* not *-ary* . . . and this is one of them.
7. intercede	The verb with the *ceed* sound ends in *cede*.
8. mirthfully	When the suffix is *-ful* plus *-ly*, there are two *l*'s.
9. monastery	This is one of only six commonplace words that ends with *-ery*, not *-ary*.
10. precede	The verb with the *ceed* sound ends in *cede*.

SO MANY RULES, SO LITTLE TIME

Parking rules, dating rules, now even spelling rules! Relax. You learned to color in the lines, didn't you? Spelling rules are a snap next to *that*. Here are three more spelling rules that can help you become a super speller.

6. Q is followed by *u*. This is a nice rule, because it has few English exceptions, one being the lightweight nylon fabric called *Qiana*. As you can imagine, this word tends not to come up much in writing (or anywhere, for that matter). *Quarter, quality, equality,* and *question* all fit the rule so nicely. Here are some more *q* words you can depend on:

iniquity	quack
quad	quadrant
quadrennial	quadriceps
quadrille	quadruplet
quaff	quagga
qualification	quark
quarry	quartz
quench	question
quetzal	quibble
quilt	quickly
quota	quotation

The rule doesn't fit with abbreviations or foreign words, however. For instance, the abbreviation for *quart* is *qt.* (not *qut.*) The east Arabia peninsula on the Persian Gulf is *Qatar*, not *Quatar*, but that's okay, because the word can also be spelled *Katar*. For ordinary English words, however, the *qu* rule is about as dependable as death and taxes.

7. Using *k*'s and *c*'s. You know it's important to mind your *p*'s and *q*'s, but did you know that as far as spelling is concerned, you're better off on the lookout for those *k*'s and *c*'s? Some words that end in *c* have a hard *k* sound. Adding *y*, *i*, or *e* after the final *c* usually changes the hard sound to a soft one, creating spelling dilemmas. As a general rule, add a *k* after the final *c* to prevent the *c* from becoming soft. Here are some examples:

Word Ending in C	Adding the K
mimic	mimicked, mimicking, mimicker
panic	panicked, panicking, panicky
picnic	picnicked, picnicking, picnicker
politic	politicking
traffic	trafficked, trafficking, trafficker

MIND YOUR P'S AND Q'S (AND A T OR TWO)

Using the rules you've learned so far in this chapter, spell each of the following words correctly and cite the rule that applies:

Word	Correct Spelling	Rule
1. qagmire		
2. mimiced		
3. qisling		
4. picniced		
5. qadriceps		
6. panicing		
7. qota		
8. trafficer		
9. qotidian		
10. politicing		

ANSWERS

Correct Spelling	Rule
1. quagmire	*q* is followed by *u*
2. mimicked	add a *k* after the final *c* or the hard sound becomes soft
3. quisling	*q* is followed by *u*
4. picnicked	add a *k* after the final *c* or the hard sound becomes soft
5. quadriceps	*q* is followed by *u*
6. panicking	add a *k* after the final *c* or the hard sound becomes soft
7. quota	*q* is followed by *u*
8. trafficker	add a *k* after the final *c* or the hard sound becomes soft
9. quotidian	*q* is followed by *u*
10. politicking	add a *k* after the final *c* or the hard sound becomes soft

THE ENGLISH SOUND **OI** IS SIMILAR TO THE SOUND OF THE LETTERS **OY** IN SPANISH, AS IN **HOY** (TODAY). THE ENGLISH SOUND **OU** IS SIMILAR TO THE SOUND OF THE LETTER **AU** IN SPANISH, AS IN **AULA** (CLASSROOM).

SPACE, THE FINAL FRONTIER

Does it seem that your hair is thinner, your waistline wider, and your spelling more open to interpretation? Well, I can't comment on your hair and waistline, but I *can* say there have been some major changes in spelling.

> IN 1877, THE INSPECTOR OF SCHOOLS IN ENGLAND NOTED THAT "OUT OF 1,972 FAILURES IN THE CIVIL SERVICE EXAMINATION, 1,866 CANDIDATES WERE ELIMINATED FOR POOR SPELLING. THAT IS, EIGHTEEN OUT OF EVERY NINETEEN WHO FAILED WERE FAILED FOR SPELLING ERRORS."

Back when you had flowing locks and a waistline worthy of Scarlett O'Hara, spelling was as dependable as ants at a picnic. Most words, even the toughest ones to spell, had just one spelling. You just looked in a dictionary and that was that. But we've gotten alternative spellings for common as well as uncommon words. Today's dictionaries are more accepting of variant spellings— misspellings, to those of us old enough to remember when Paul McCartney was a member of the Beatles.

Today, some spellings are carved in sand, not granite. No matter how reputable the different dictionaries may be, they can differ substantially when it comes to variant spellings. According to current estimates, there are variant spellings for more than 2,000 words. One of the major sticking points facing the poor folks who make our dictionaries concerns space: If a word is hyphenated, should it be closed up or written as two separate words: *re-examine* or *reexamine*? *coordinate* or *co-ordinate*?

Spelling involves not only letters but also spaces, to say nothing of hyphens. This is the problem you face with compound words, those words made of two or more smaller words. For example, is it *snow ball, snow-ball,* or *snowball*? What about *paper clip? paperclip? paper-clip*? Look at them long enough and they all look wrong. (Inquiring minds want to know: *snowball* is one word, *paper clip* is two.)

Compound words fall into three categories: *open compounds, closed compounds, hyphenated compounds.* Here are the definitions and examples:

1. *Open compounds* are written as two words:
       cedar shingles
       executive secretary
       night shift

2. *Closed compounds* are written as one word:

> handbook
> homemaker
> northeast

> SOME WORDS BEGIN THEIR LIVES WITHOUT A HYPHEN, ADOPT ONE, AND THEN DROP IT. **STEAMBOAT**, FOR EXAMPLE, WAS ONCE **STEAM BOAT**, THEN **STEAM-BOAT**.

3. *Hyphenated compounds* have that little hyphen:

> comparison-contrast
> nurse-practitioner
> secretary-treasurer

DOING THE TWO-STEP

Try your hand at the following compound words. Circle the ones that you think are spelled correctly. May the force be with you.

1. tail light	taillight	tail-light
2. student union	studentunion	student-union
3. tractor trailer	tractortrailer	tractor-trailer
4. step ladder	stepladder	step-ladder
5. book keeper	bookkeeper	book-keeper
6. locker room	lockerroom	locker-room
7. Italian American	ItalianAmerican	Italian-American
8. night club	nightclub	night-club
9. father in law	fatherinlaw	father-in-law
10. toll booth	tollbooth	toll-booth
11. window sill	windowsill	window-sill
12. bow tie	bowtie	bow-tie
13. bar bell	barbell	bar-bell
14. hair shirt	hairshirt	hair-shirt
15. twenty page	twentypage	twenty-page
16. cream puff	creampuff	cream-puff
17. sales clerk	salesclerk	sales-clerk
18. hammer lock	hammerlock	hammer-lock
19. fast paced	fastpaced	fast-paced
20. back seat	backseat	back-seat

ANSWERS

1. taillight
2. student union
3. tractor-trailer
4. stepladder
5. bookkeeper
6. locker room
7. Italian-American
8. nightclub
9. father-in-law
10. tollbooth
11. windowsill
12. bow tie
13. barbell
14. hair shirt
15. twenty-page
16. creampuff
17. salesclerk
18. hammerlock
19. fast-paced
20. backseat

THE FOLLOWING WORDS ARE
ALL CLOSED COMPOUNDS:
**WASTEWATER,
FILMMAKER,
POTHOLDER, BIRDBATH,
PASSIONFLOWER,
LANDOWNER,
GALLBLADDER,
LAWSUIT.**

A HYPHEN IS ONE CLICK OF
THE BUTTON (-);
A DASH IS TWO (—).
A HYPHEN IS USED WITHIN
WORDS; A DASH IS USED
BETWEEN WORDS.

CHAPTER 5

*D*OUBLE TROUBLE:

HOMONYMS AND HOMOPHONES

YOU MUST REMEMBER THIS

Words with the same pronunciation but different spellings and meanings *(homophones)* present special spelling challenges. So do words with the same spelling and pronunciation but different meanings *(homonyms)*.

ALL THE RIGHT MOVES

Use a dictionary to verify that you have the word you want—not its *homonym* or *homophone*.

ARE YOU ALREADY (OR IS THAT ALL READY)?

Experienced speakers and readers of English have learned the basic connections between sounds and letter combinations that enable them to spell a large number of words. So far, so good. But what happens when two words sound the same, but are spelled differently and have different meanings? English even has groups of *three* words that sound the same, but are spelled differently and have different meanings. This dilemma has resulted in one of the most common causes of spelling confusion.

Frequently, certain pairs of words are confused, misused, and misspelled. Sometimes it is because the words sound alike; other times it is because they are spelled alike but carry different meanings. In either event, distinguishing between these confusing words is crucial because it helps you write exactly what you mean. Therefore, keeping these words straight can help you avoid needless embarrassment.

The prime offenders are called *homophones* and

homonyms. *Homophones* are words with the same pronunciation but different spellings and meanings, such as *coarse* and *course* or *bridal* and *bridle*. *Homonyms* are words with the same spelling and pronunciation but different meanings, such as *bay* and *bay* and *beam* and *beam*. In general, homophones are more commonplace than homonyms.

Unfortunately, there aren't a lot of mnemonics to help you distinguish between these word pairs and triads. In this chapter, you'll learn the most useful memory devices, but the rest of the words can only be learned through memorization.

> **WEAR** MEANS "TO USE FOR CLOTHING;" **WHERE** INDICATES PLACE.

First, let's see where you stand before we decide where you have to go. Complete each of the following sentences by circling the correct word. Some sentences may have more than one word to be circled.

1. The total weight of all insects on earth is twelve times greater (than, then) the weight of all people.

2. The shrimp's heart is in (its, it's) head.

3. In the Arctic, the (sun, son) sometimes appears to (bee, be) square.

4. Because they (our, are) on opposite sides of the San Andreas Fault, Los Angeles and San Francisco become 2.5 inches closer together each year.

5. Up to 3,000 species of trees have been found in (won, one) square mile of the Amazon jungle.

6. When North America was first settled, beavers (their, they're, there) grew to the size of (bears, bares).

7. Worldwide, about forty square miles of land are transformed into (dessert, desert) each day.

8. In 1859, twenty-four rabbits were released in Australia. Within six years, the population increased by (too, to, two) million.

9. Some elephants have been known to remain standing after they have (dyed, died).

10. All office-seekers in the Roman Empire were obliged to (ware, wear) a certain white toga for a period of one year before the election.

ANSWERS	
1. than	6. there, bears
2. its	7. desert
3. sun, be	8. two
4. are	9. died
5. one	10. wear

NATURE CALLS

Some people find it easier to remember spelling words when they are grouped around a common theme. Here, then, are often confused word pairs and trios loosely grouped around the theme of animals and the natural world.

1. *base*: the bottom part of an object; the plate in baseball; morally low
   "Put the lamp <u>base</u> by the fireplace," the decorator said.

   bass: a type of fish; the lowest male voice; a musical instrument
   The fisherman was thrilled when he reeled in a huge <u>bass</u>.

2. *bare*: not dressed; unadorned, plain
   The toddler liked to take off his diaper and run around <u>bare</u>.

   bear: a carnivorous or omnivorous mammal of the family *Ursidae*, having a massive body, coarse fur, and short limbs
   When President Theodore Roosevelt refused to kill a baby <u>bear</u>, a new toy craze was born.

   bear: carry, hold
   I <u>bear</u> no grudges; I forgive and forget.

> USE THIS MNEMONIC TO DISTINGUISH BETWEEN **DESSERT** AND **DESERT**: **DESSERT**, THE SWEET AT THE END OF A MEAL, HAS TWO **S**'S FOR A SECOND SERVING.

3. *boar*: male pig

> The old <u>boar</u> was king of the farmyard; all the other animals respected him.

  bore: tiresome person

> A <u>bore</u> is someone who, when you ask him how he is, tells you.

4. *born*: native, brought forth by birth

> <u>Born</u> free; live free.

  borne: endured (past participle of "to bear")

> A century ago, men would duel when they had <u>borne</u> an insult to their honor.

5. *cheap*: not expensive

> Talk is <u>cheap</u> because supply exceeds demand.

  cheep: sound a young bird makes.

> "<u>Cheep</u>!" said the newborn bluejay.

6. *dear*: beloved

> We use the term <u>dear</u> to indicate that a person is much loved.

  deer: animal

> The <u>deer</u> flicked its beautiful white tail and bounded away.

7. *died*: ceased living

> The little boy cried for days after his pet frog <u>died</u>.

  dyed: changed color

> The makeover was a disaster; the woman's hair was accidentally <u>dyed</u> purple.

8. *gorilla*: ape

> Washoe, a <u>gorilla</u>, learned to "speak" in sign language.

  guerrilla: soldier

> The <u>guerrilla</u> was armed and ready to fight for his country's honor.

9. *leach*: to dissolve through percolation
You can <u>leach</u> impurities from water by using filters.

leech: a bloodsucking worm
In medieval times, doctors sometimes used <u>leeches</u> as a medical treatment.

10. *meat*: animal flesh
Vegetarians will not eat any <u>meat</u>.

> **GUILT** AND **GILT** SOUND THE SAME BUT HAVE WIDELY DIFFERENT MEANINGS. **GUILT** MEANS A FEELING OF REMORSE; **GILT** IS A THIN GOLD COVERING.

meet: to encounter; to assemble
You can often <u>meet</u> nice people in school, in church, and doing volunteer work for the community.

11. *reed*: straight stalks of any tall marsh grass
We like to dry the <u>reeds</u> and make them into table decorations.

read: interpret the written word
John F. Kennedy could <u>read</u> very quickly; he often devoured an entire book in a single day.

PROGRESS CHECK

Take a break (not a *brake*) and complete the following quiz by selecting the correct definition for each spelling word. Write the letter of your choice in the space provided.

_____ 1. boar
    a. female pig   c. suffer
    b. male pig   d. tiresome person

_____ 2. guerrilla
    a. soldier   c. monkey
    b. ape   d. primate

_____ 3. borne
    a. brought forth by birth   c. native
    b. survived   d. endured

_____ 4. cheep
    a. economical   c. loud
    b. paltry   d. what a young bird says

_____ 5. meet
    a. give out   c. encounter; assemble
    b. food   d. animal flesh

_____ 6. deer
    a. worshipped   c. beloved
    b. reviled   d. animal

_____ 7. leech
    a. bloodsucking worm   c. killer
    b. dissolve   d. slimy

_____ 8. cheap
    a. bird sound   c. not expensive
    b. bound   d. consume

_____ 9. bear
    a. friend   c. born
    b. large animal   d. support

_____ 10. read
    a. interpret written words   c. sow
    b. tall marsh grass   d. plants

AN **ALTAR** IS A PLATFORM UPON WHICH RELIGIOUS RITES ARE PERFORMED. **ALTER**, IN CONTRAST, MEANS "TO CHANGE."

ANSWERS

1. b	6. d
2. a	7. a
3. d	8. c
4. d	9. b
5. c	10. a

BUYING AND SELLING

Below are ten often misspelled word pairs that have to do with business and commerce. Use a dictionary to help you define each word and use it in a sentence. (Don't panic; answers follow.)

1. sell _____
    cell _____

2. cent _____
    scent _____

3. do _____
    due _____

4. buy _____
    by _____

5. capital_____
    Capitol _____

6. fare _____
    fair _____

7. allot _____
    a lot _____

8. site _____
    sight _____

9. principle_____
    principal_____

10. bread _____
    bred _____

ANSWERS

1. sell: to trade
   cell: a small room, as in a convent or a prison
2. cent: a penny
   scent: aroma
3. do: to act or make (verb)
   due: caused by (adjective)
4. buy: to purchase
   by: near or next to
5. capital: net worth of a business; the city or town that is the official seat of government; highly important
   Capitol: any building in which a legislature meets
6. fare: the price charged for transporting a passenger or goods
   fair: not biased; moderately large; moderately good
7. allot: to divide
   a lot: many
8. site: place
   sight: vision
9. principle: rule
   principal: head of a school; main
10. bread: baked goods
    bred: to cause to be born (past participle of "to breed")

HOMO SAPIENS

Now let's turn our gaze inward and look at ourselves. Below are ten often misspelled word pairs that have to do with human behavior. As you read through these words, see how many you might have misspelled in the past.

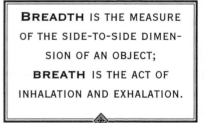

BREADTH IS THE MEASURE OF THE SIDE-TO-SIDE DIMENSION OF AN OBJECT; **BREATH** IS THE ACT OF INHALATION AND EXHALATION.

1. *air*: atmosphere
   There's no <u>air</u> in a vacuum.

   err: make a mistake
   To <u>err</u> is human; to forgive, divine.

2. *all together*: all at one time
   We have to attend the meeting <u>all together</u>.

altogether: completely

He was <u>altogether</u> flabbergasted by the astonishing turn of events.

3. *allowed*: given permission

The teenager was upset that he was not <u>allowed</u> to attend the unchaperoned party.

aloud: out loud, verbally

Shhh! Don't say it <u>aloud</u>!

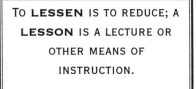

To **LESSEN** IS TO REDUCE; A **LESSON** IS A LECTURE OR OTHER MEANS OF INSTRUCTION.

4. *bored*: not interested

The new television show <u>bored</u> us.

board: a thin piece of wood; a group of directors

We needed a sturdy <u>board</u> to support the wedding cake.

5. *bridal*: pertaining to the bride or a wedding

The <u>bridal</u> party assembled on the lawn.

bridle: part of a horse's harness

The groom shined the horse's <u>bridle</u> until it gleamed.

6. *conscience*: moral sense

Living with a <u>conscience</u> is like driving a car with the brakes on.

conscious: awake

The patient was soon <u>conscious</u> after the operation.

7. *glutinous*: sticky

The rice was so <u>glutinous</u> that it stuck to our hands.

gluttonous: eating voraciously

The <u>gluttonous</u> family consumed 15 chickens, 10 pounds of french fries, and 5 cakes at one sitting.

8. *right*: correct

He who hesitates is probably <u>right</u>.

write: to form letters
The child learned to write in the second grade.

9. *vain*: egotistical
The woman was so <u>vain</u> that she could not pass a mirror without checking her appearance.

vane: a device that shows wind direction
According to the weather vane, the wind is coming from the south.

vein: a narrow water channel; blood vessel
The nurse had trouble finding a suitable <u>vein</u> in my arm for a shot.

10. *whine*: complain
The child could <u>whine</u> for hours without taking a break.

wine: fermented grape juice
The vineyards produced their first crop of <u>wine</u> this season.

VILE MEANS "HATEFUL"; A **VIAL** IS A SLIM CONTAINER.

MIX 'N' MATCH

Match each of the following spelling words to its meaning. Write the letter of the correct answer in the space provided.

_____ 1. bridle	a. atmosphere
_____ 2. altogether	b. device showing wind direction
_____ 3. conscious	c. given permission
_____ 4. right	d. part of a horse's harness
_____ 5. whine	e. pertaining to a wedding
_____ 6. gluttonous	f. verbally
_____ 7. allowed	g. awake
_____ 8. vain	h. a thin piece of wood
_____ 9. err	i. completely
_____ 10. wine	j. fermented grape juice
_____ 11. all together	k. sticky
_____ 12. board	l. correct

_____ 13. vane	m. make a mistake
_____ 14. bored	n. to form letters
_____ 15. conscience	o. moral sense
_____ 16. aloud	p. complain
_____ 17. write	q. egotistical
_____ 18. glutinous	r. all at one time
_____ 19. air	s. not interested
_____ 20. bridal	t. eating voraciously

ANSWERS

1. d	11. r
2. i	12. h
3. g	13. b
4. l	14. s
5. p	15. o
6. t	16. f
7. c	17. n
8. q	18. k
9. m	19. a
10. j	20. e

MIRROR IMAGES

Supply the homophone for each of these confusing pairs of spelling words. Select your answers from the words in the box. Then write your answer in the space provided.

there, they're	heir	rote
piece	hart	ours
shear	phase	presents
for	soul	grate
hear	its	made

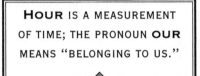

HOUR IS A MEASUREMENT OF TIME; THE PRONOUN **OUR** MEANS "BELONGING TO US."

1. faze _____

2. fore _____

3. great _____

4. hair _____

5. here _____

6. hours _____

7. it's _____

8. their _____ and _____

9. maid _____

10. peace _____

11. sheer _____

12. presence _____

13. heart _____

14. wrote _____

15. sole _____

ANSWERS

1. phase	6. ours	11. shear
2. four	7. its	12. presents
3. grate	8. there, they're	13. hart
4. heir	9. made	14. rote
5. hear	10. piece	15. soul

SEE THE WORLD

Below are ten pairs of often misspelled words that have to do with travel. Read the definitions and spell the words in your head to make sure you've got these tricky traveling words down cold.

1. *ark*: boat

> Noah's <u>ark</u> housed two creatures of each species.

  arc: part of the circumference of a circle; curved line.

> You can measure an <u>arc</u> with a compass.

2. *berth*: a sleeping area in a ship

> On the cruise, the first-class <u>berth</u> cost twice as much as the budget one.

  birth: being born

> Today, many fathers are present at the <u>birth</u> of their children. However, this was not commonplace a generation ago.

3. *plane*: airplane

> Today's <u>planes</u> come equipped with telephones and video games—and they can even fly you long distances for a moderate cost.

  plain: not beautiful; obvious

> Sophia Loren was a <u>plain</u> child who grew up to be a beautiful woman.

4. *bow*: the forward end of a ship; to bend from the waist; a device used to propel arrows; loops of ribbon

> "Please step to the <u>bow</u> of the ship," the captain said during the lifeboat drill.

beau: sweetheart
> Nancy's <u>beau</u> brought her a dozen red roses.

5. *brake*: a device for slowing a vehicle
> Many people <u>brake</u> for animals.

  break: to crack or destroy
> The vase will <u>break</u> if you drop it.

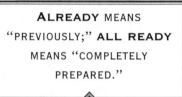

A **GRANDAM** IS A GRANDMOTHER; A **GRANDE DAME** IS AN IMPOSING WOMAN.

6. *ascent:* to move up
> The plane's <u>ascent</u> was surprisingly smooth.

  assent: to agree
> <u>Assent</u> to our plan if you have nothing better to suggest.

7. *hangar*: an airplane garage
> The pilot carefully maneuvered the plane into the <u>hangar</u>.

  hanger: a wire implement for hanging clothing in a closet
> Have you ever noticed how wire <u>hangers</u> seem to multiply in your closet?

ALREADY MEANS "PREVIOUSLY;" **ALL READY** MEANS "COMPLETELY PREPARED."

8. *stationary*: fixed
> The cat, absolutely <u>stationary</u>, stared at the bird.

  stationery: writing paper
> Many professionals have fine, embossed <u>stationery</u>.

9. *flew*: past tense of "to fly"
> The jet <u>flew</u> through the air.

  flue: fireplace exhaust pipe
> We opened the <u>flue</u> on the fireplace to let the smoke escape.

10. *led*: past tense of "to lead"
> A Los Angeles man, who later said he was "tired of walking," stole a

steamroller and <u>led</u> police on a five-mile-per-hour chase until an officer stepped aboard and brought the vehicle to a stop.

lead: to conduct; bluish-gray metal
The tour guide <u>leads</u> us through the museum.

LAST LICKS

Here's one last quiz to catch some additional tough spelling words and to review some you've already learned in this lesson. Circle the correct word to complete each sentence.

1. To keep from being separated while sleeping, sea otters tie themselves together with kelp, often drifting miles out to (see, sea) during the night.

> THE COMBINATION OF LETTERS **OUGH** CAN BE PRONOUNCED IN NINE DIFFERENT WAYS. THE FOLLOWING SENTENCE CONTAINS THEM ALL: "A ROUGH-COATED, DOUGH-FACED, THOUGHTFUL PLOUGHMAN STRODE THROUGH THE STREETS OF SCARBOROUGH; AFTER FALLING INTO A SLOUGH, HE COUGHED AND HICCOUGHED."

2. Students at U.S. colleges and universities (reed, read) about 60,000 pages in (for, four) years.

3. (Their, There, They're) is enough stone in the (Grate, Great) Wall of China to build an eight-foot wall circling the globe at the equator.

4. The bacteria found on human skin (our, are) roughly the numerical equivalent of all the humans on earth.

5. A cockroach can live for several weeks without (it's, its) head.

6. The brightest star in the sky, Sirius, gives out twenty-six times as much light as the (son, sun.)

7. Mosquitoes are attracted to (blew, blue) more than any other color.

8. Mosquitoes have killed more people (then, than) have all the world's wars combined.

9. The telephone was fifty-one years old before (one, won) was installed on the desk of the President of the United States.

10. In 1936, U.S. track star Jesse Owens (beet, beat) a racehorse over a 100-yard course. The horse was given a head start.

11. (Do, Due) to the reclining S shape of the Isthmus of Panama, the sun rises on the Pacific Coast and sets on the Atlantic Coast in the Isthmus of Panama.

12. When tea was first introduced in the American colonies, many people, not knowing what to do with the stuff, served the tea leaves with sugar or syrup and (threw, through) away the water they had been boiled in.

13. The temperature in eastern Siberia can get so cold that the moisture in a person's breath can freeze in the (heir, air) and fall to the ground.

14. Worldwide, there are more statues of Joan of (Ark, Arc) than of anyone else. France alone has about 40,000 of them.

15. In eighteenth-century France, visitors to the royal palace in Versailles were allowed to stand in a roped-off section of the (mane, main) dining room and watch the king and queen eat.

16. A lifetime supply of all the vitamins you need (ways, weighs) only about eight ounces.

17. The candidate (whose, who's) tie was striped got more votes than his competitor.

18. When opossums are "playing possum," they are not playing. They actually pass out from (shear, sheer) terror.

19. The main library at Indiana University sinks more than an inch every year, because when it was built engineers failed to take into account the weight of all the books that (wood, would) occupy the building.

20. Before thermometers were invented, brewers would dip a thumb into the mix to find the right temperature for adding yeast. (To, Two, Too) cold and the yeast wouldn't grow. (To, Two, Too) hot and the yeast would die. This is where we get the phrase "rule of thumb."

ANSWERS

1. sea	11. Due
2. read, four	12. threw
3. There, Great	13. air
4. are	14. Arc
5. its	15. main
6. sun	16. weighs
7. blue	17. whose
8. than	18. sheer
9. one	19. would
10. beat	20. Too, Too

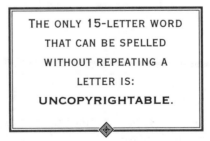

THE ONLY 15-LETTER WORD
THAT CAN BE SPELLED
WITHOUT REPEATING A
LETTER IS:
UNCOPYRIGHTABLE.

CHAPTER 6

$\mathscr{S}$SSHHH!

TIPS FOR FINDING SILENT LETTERS

> ### YOU MUST REMEMBER THIS
> Silent letters can fool even the best spellers.
>
> ### ALL THE RIGHT MOVES
> Say the silent letter to yourself to help you remember to include it, as in *dumb*, *gnaw*, and *empty*.

A little boy was overheard talking to himself as he strode through his backyard, baseball cap in place and toting the ball and bat. "I'm the greatest baseball player in the world," he said proudly. Then he tossed the ball in the air, swung, and missed. Undaunted, he picked up the ball, threw it into the air, and said to himself, "I'm the greatest baseball player ever!" He swung at the ball again, and again he missed. He paused a moment to examine the bat and ball carefully. Then once again he threw the ball into the air and said, "I'm the greatest baseball player who ever lived."

He swung the bat hard and again missed the ball. "Wow!" he exclaimed. "What a pitcher!"

Confidence is a wonderful thing, but not when it comes to spelling words with silent letters. Some words with silent letters can trick even the most experienced spellers. In this chapter, you'll learn which words present the greatest challenges—and why.

COVERT OPERATIONS: SILENT LETTERS

Never seem to meet the people you want to get to know, but can't get rid of the same old pests? The same is true of spelling words. Keeping this truism in mind, here are some words with silent letters that have no doubt been annoying you for years. Only now, you know why.

> TODAY, THE TYPOGRAPHICAL COUNCIL FOR SPELLING REFORM ADVOCATES THE SO-CALLED "SOUNDSPELL" ALPHABETICAL SYSTEM. DON'T HOLD YOUR BREATH WAITING FOR THE NEW SYSTEM TO BE ADOPTED.

Many words contain silent letters, such as the *k* and *w* in *know* or the *b* in *dumb* or letters that are not frequently pronounced in everyday speech, such as the first *r* in *February*. What do you want first: the good news or the bad news?

Here's the bad news: the easiest way to learn these words is to commit them to memory. Want the good news? See the bad news.

The following words each contain a silent letter—a letter that is seen but not heard. Be extra careful to include it when you spell the word.

1. **Silent b.** The silent *b* is small but deadly. Most of us are familiar with the silent *b* at the end of a word (as in *comb*), but Mr. B is a subtle letter that can occur even in the middle of a word (as in plum*b*er). Here are some of the most common words in which the *b* hides:

climb	comb
crumb	debt
doubt	dumb
plumber	redoubtable
subpoena	subtle
thumb	undoubtedly

2. **Silent c.** The silent *c* can be even harder to find than the silent *b* because it doesn't tend to stick out as much. Here are some words that contain the silent *c*. How many of them have you had difficulty spelling?

acquaint	acquire
acquit	ascertain

corpuscle	czar
descend	fascinate
indict	miscellaneous
muscle	scent
scissors	

3. Silent d. Fortunately, there are very few words with a silent *d*. However, it will be just your luck to have to spell one of them in an important document.

> all *adj* words, such as *adjoin*
> handkerchief

4. Silent g. This one is especially tricky because the silent *g* can crop up when you least expect it, as in the words *diaphragm* and *align*. Here is a list of the most frequently misspelled words that contain a silent *g*:

> align
> design
> gnarled
> gnaw
> gnome

5. Silent h. *Rhyme* and *rhythm* are very often misspelled because of the silent *h*; only the brave tackle such silent *h* words as *rheumatism, exhilaration,* and *gingham.* After this lesson, however, you'll sneer at such spelling wimps.

exhaust	exhibit
forehead	ghastly
ghetto	ghost
gingham	heir
herb	rhetoric
rhyme	rhythm
shepherd	spaghetti
vehicle	

SILENT, BUT DEADLY

Each of the following words is spelled correctly. To help you remember the correct spellings, circle the silent letter in each word.

1. acquire
2. adjoin
3. corpuscle
4. czar
5. doubt

6. handkerchief
7. miscellaneous
8. redoubtable
9. subpoena
10. subtle

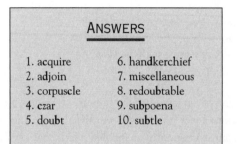

ANSWERS

1. acquire
2. adjoin
3. corpuscle
4. czar
5. doubt

6. handkerchief
7. miscellaneous
8. redoubtable
9. subpoena
10. subtle

6. Silent k. This one's a snap if you remember to be on the lookout for words with the *kn* combination.

> all -*kn* words, such as *knack* and *knob*
> acknowledge

7. Silent l. Look for the *alm* pattern and you shouldn't find silent *l* such a villain. Here are some examples that crop up frequently in written documents:

> almond   balm
> calm   folk
> half   salmon
> talk   walk
> would

8. Silent m. There's only one frequently used word—*mnemonic*—and you have a mnemonic for it anyway.

> mnemonic

9. Silent n. Again, look for patterns. With the silent *n*, you'll find the culprit most often hanging out at the end of words, as in these examples:

> autumn   column
> condemn   damn
> hymn   solemn

10. **Silent *p*.** This one's as nasty as a frustrated shopper. Watch for hidden *p*'s in the beginning, middle, and end of a word. Sort of like looking for bargains in all the right places. Here are some examples:

corps (the *s* is silent, too)	cupboard
pneumatic	pneumonia
psalm	
pseudonym	
psychology	
ptomaine	
receipt	

> PALINDROMES ARE WORDS THAT CAN BE READ THE SAME FORWARD AND BACKWARD, SUCH AS **POP** AND **REDIVIDER**.

SNEAKY PEAK

Match each misspelled word to its correct spelling. Write the letter of the correct spelling in the space provided.

_____1. alin	a. autumn
_____2. gastly	b. knack
_____3. exilaration	c. almond
_____4. acnowledge	d. would
_____5. amond	e. align
_____6. narled	f. exhibit
_____7. gingam	g. acknowledge
_____8. autum	h. ghastly
_____9. tomaine	i. condemn
_____10. condem	j. gnarled
_____11. woud	k. design
_____12. spagetti	l. exhilaration
_____13. desin	m. ptomaine
_____14. nack	n. gingham
_____15. exibit	o. spaghetti

ANSWERS		
1. e	6. j	11. d
2. h	7. n	12. o
3. l	8. a	13. k
4. g	9. m	14. b
5. c	10. i	15. f

(Back to work: Tote that barge! Lift that bale! Find that hidden letter.)

11. Silent *s*. Sneaky like a snake, the silent *s* can appear anywhere in a word. In some words, such as *island*, you'll recognize something is wrong because the word will look "funny"; in other cases, you might not even be aware that the word's misspelled (as in *viscount)*.

aisle	corps (the *p* is silent, too)
debris	lisle
Louisville	rendezvous

12. Silent *t*. Most often, the silent *t* will be smack dab in the middle of the word, as in *listen, stretch,* and *whistle*. This makes it relatively easy to find. Here are some additional examples that you're likely to encounter in your writing adventures:

bankruptcy	Christmas
mortgage	mustn't
wrestle	

13. Silent *u*. Look for the *gu* combination; it's the most common place to find a silent *u*. Check out these examples:

bodyguard	guardian
guarantee	guess
guest	guide
lifeguard	

14. Silent *w*. Not hard to find in a word such as *sword* or *wrap*, but a killer when it comes to *playwright*. You'd be surprised how often people misspell *wr* words, such as *write*.

all *wr* words, such as *write*   answer
two   whole

SSSHHH!

Each of the following words is misspelled because it is missing a silent letter. Correct each misspelled word by providing the silent letter. Then write the word correctly, in the space provided.

1. diaphram

2. tomaine

3. getto

4. redoutable

5. zar

6. vicount

7. reumatism

8. misellaneous

9. neumonia

10. supoena

ANSWERS

1. diaphragm   6. viscount
2. ptomaine   7. rheumatism
3. ghetto   8. miscellaneous
4. redoubtable   9. pneumonia
5. czar   10. subpoena

BAD SPELLERS OF THE
WORLD, UNTIE!

PROOF ME

Fortunately, third grade is long past and Miss Shultz can't call on you to spell "macaroni" or "vacuum" during one of those cursed spelling bees. In fact, probably the only time you have to spell a word aloud is when your kid yells out, "How do you spell *pineapple?*" Then you can always gleefully shout, "Look it up, Junior. Then you'll remember it."

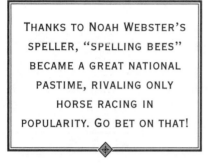

THANKS TO NOAH WEBSTER'S SPELLER, "SPELLING BEES" BECAME A GREAT NATIONAL PASTIME, RIVALING ONLY HORSE RACING IN POPULARITY. GO BET ON THAT!

But you *do* have to know how to spell when you write at home and on the job. You also have to know how to spell when you proofread your own and someone else's documents. There's no faking it here.

In this chapter, you learned tips for finding silent letters. Let's expand that to include proofreading for spelling errors. How good is your eye for misspellings when they appear in a printed passage? Read the following passage and circle all the misspelled words. Then spell the words correctly in the spaces provided. Look for homonyms, silent letters, and missing letters. Don't forget to apply spelling rules, too. Check the answer key for your score.

THE "BLACK SOX" SCANDAL

Their have been many controvercial World Series, but the most imfamous was certainly the throne World Series of 1919. Even though the White Sox were favored 5 to 1, about $2 millon had bet on the Cincinnati Reds to win. Sensing a sure thing, Jack Doyle, the head of a New York City beting ring, rigged the series. Actually, the series seemed quiet respectable, with the Reds winning it five games to three. For this reason, very few people suspected the players had been bought. Neverless, the very next day sportswriter Hugh Fullerton suggested that something was not quite right. As a result of Fullerton's suggestion, the owner of the White Sox, Charles Cominsky, offered a cash reward to anyone who could prove a fix. It took all most a year for three men—Lefty Williams, Eddie Cicotte, and J. Jackson—to sign confessions admitting the series had been fixed and they were in on it. But just before the trail was scheduled to start, the confessions mysteriously vanished from the office of the Illinois state attorney. When the case was finally tried, the three men denied having made any confessions and having been involved in any way in the rigging scheme because there was no proof against them.

1. _____
2. _____
3. _____
4. _____
5. _____
6. _____
7. _____
8. _____
9. _____
10. _____

ANSWERS

1. There
2. controversial
3. infamous
4. thrown
5. million

6. betting
7. quite
8. Nevertheless
9. almost
10. trial

✔ SCORE YOURSELF

18 or more	Go to the head of the class, Hawkeye.
17–14	You'd get picked for the spelling bee.
13–10	On the right track.
9–6	Less television would be a good start.
5–0	We should talk. And soon.

"TAKE CARE THAT YOU NEVER SPELL A WORD WRONG. ALWAYS BEFORE YOU WRITE A WORD, CONSIDER HOW IT IS SPELLED, AND IF YOU DO NOT REMEMBER, TURN TO A DICTIONARY. IT PRODUCES GREAT PRAISE TO SPELL WELL."

(THOMAS JEFFERSON)

Try it again with the following paragraph. Read the passage, circle all the misspelled words, and spell the words correctly in the spaces provided.

THE GREAT POTATO FAMINE IN IRELAND

The potatoe has had a major historical inpact on the country of Ireland. In the eighteenth and nintheenth centurys, the average Irish citizen planted potatoes and ate about ten pounds of potatoes a day—and little else. Potatoes are nourishing: on this deit, the Irish population nearly tripled from the middle of the eighteenth century to just about the middle of the nineteenth century. But depending on only one food was dangerous. When the potato blite hit Europe in 1845, the results were devestating in Ireland. In Ireland, the potato famine meant more than starvation that year. It meant no sede potatoes to use to grow the next year's crop. It meant that the pig or cow that would usaully have been sold to pay the rent had to be slaughtered, because there was nothing to faten it on. No pig or cow meant no rent. No rent meant eviction. As a result, homelessness and disease followed on the heels of hunger. Almost a million Irish people died as a result of the potato blight. Another million moved to the United States.

1. _____
2. _____
3. _____
4. _____
5. _____
6. _____
7. _____
8. _____
9. _____
10. _____

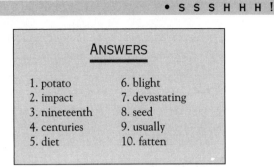

Once more for good luck. (You know that three's the charm.) Read the passage, circle all the misspelled words, and spell the words correctly in the spaces provided.

A NIGHT TO REMEMBER

Just before midnight on April 14, 1912, one of the most dramatic and famous of all maritime disasters occured, the sinking of the *Titanic*. The *Titanic* was the most luxurious ship afloat at the time, with it's beautifully decorated staterooms, glitering crystal chandeleirs, and elaborate food service. In addition, it was supposed to be the safest ocean liner ever built. The hull of the 46,000-ton White Star liner was divided into sixteen supposedly watertihgt compartments. According to the ship's manufacturer, four of the sixteen compartments could be flooded without threatening the ship's boyancy. That April, the magestic ocean liner was on its first voyage ever, travveling from Southampton, England, to New York City. The evening of April 14, the ship was sailing 95 miles south of Newfundland when it collided with a gigantic iceberg. No one saw the iceberg until it was only about 500 yards away, a distance the ship would travel in 37 seconds. The ship sunk because the iceberg ruptured five of the sixteen watertight compartments. The "unsinkable" *Titanic* vanished under the water at 2:20 A.M., April 15. There were about 2,200 passengers aboard, and all but 678 died. The tradgedy was made even worse by the crew's futile rescue attempts. Since there were not enough lifeboats, hundreds of people died who could have survived.

1. _____

2. _____

3. _____

4. _____

5. _____

6. _____

7. _____

8. _____

9. _____

10. _____

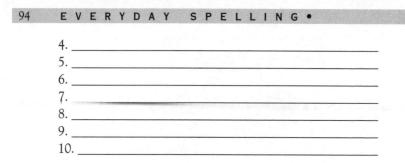

ANSWERS

1. occurred
2. its
3. glittering
4. chandeliers
5. watertight
6. buoyancy
7. majestic
8. traveling
9. Newfoundland
10. tragedy

CHAPTER 7

$\mathscr{S}$ILENT BUT DEADLY:

UNPHONETIC WORDS

YOU MUST REMEMBER THIS
Some words are unphonetic; they don't sound the way they are spelled.

ALL THE RIGHT MOVES
There's no choice here; just take a deep breath, square your shoulders, and memorize the words.

How do you spell any one of the denizens of the deep, such as a flounder, bass, trout, sturgeon, carp, or even the lowly gold? This is a snap, you're thinking. It's *f-i-s-h*. Not so fast, Kemosabe. Did you know that fish can also be spelled *ghotti? Ghotti?!* Here's how.

> Take the . . .
> *gh* as in *tough*,
> *o* as in *women*,
> *ti* as in *action*,
> and you get "*f-i-s-h*" (or *ghotti*, as it's also spelled).

And that's not all. Consider that . . .

- the sound of the letter *g*, as in *get*, can be spelled *gh*, as in *ghost*;
- the sound of the letter *h*, as in *how*, can be spelled *wh*, as in *who*;
- the sound of the letter *j*, as in *jug*, can be spelled *g*, as in *gentle*;
- the sound of the letter *k*, as in *keg*, can be spelled *c*, as in *cap*, or *ch*, as in *chemistry*;

- the sound of the letter *r*, as in *rug*, can be spelled *wr*, as in *wrong*;
- the sound of the letter combination *sh*, as in *shy*, is spelled *s*, as in *sugar*.

The spelling of a word as it appears within parentheses in a dictionary is called its *phonetic* spelling. In the *phonetic alphabet*, letters and symbols represent the sound of the word as you say it.

> I'D LIKE YOU TO THINK I'M OFFERING YOU SOMETHING UNIQUE HERE, BUT EVERY DICTIONARY WORTH ITS NAME CONTAINS A PRONUNCIATION KEY. IT'S USUALLY LOCATED IN THE FRONT OF THE BOOK.

SEE AND SAY

To make sure we're all singing from the same hymnal, let's start with a pronunciation key. For simplicity's sake, I've given only one pronunciation for each word. Nonetheless, variant pronunciations are often acceptable (just to make your life a little more confusing).

PRONUNCIATION KEY

å	mat, parry	o	opt, mom
Å	aim, ray	o	own, growth, no
a	air, wary	o	morbid, tall, ought
a	ah, calm	oi	oink, toy
b	bond, rabid, slab	oo	look
ch	chair, bachelor	oo	ooze, boot
d	die, cad	ou	ouch, scow
e	lend	p	put, slipper
e	emit, squeal, only	r	rate, barracks
f	fat, ruffle	s	sail, truss
g	wig, slugger	sh	shine, ocean, push
h	hint	t	tall, otter
hw	which	th	thanks, either
i	inn	th	then, other
i	ire, defy	u	uncle, mud
j	joke, hedge	u(r)	urn, burr
k	key, lack	v	vend, lover

l	i**ll**, **l**ost, fe**ll**ow	w	**w**ilt, a**w**ake
m	**m**y, si**mm**er	y	**y**ellow, can**y**on
n	**n**ew, ru**nn**er	z	ea**s**y, **z**oo
ng	wi**ng**	zh	mea**s**ure, gara**g**e
ə	vowel in an unstressed syllable as in **a**ttend, po**e**m, loc**u**st, Connecticut		

You'll notice that some of the vowels have marks over them. These are called *diacritical marks*. They tell you the sound the vowel has in the word.

Now, phonetics is a great concept, right up there with late-night television, lite beer, and microwave popcorn. Phonetics works well when the words are cooperative and follow the rules, being spelled the way they sound. Unfortunately, some words just refuse to cooperate.

As a result, many words are frequently misspelled because they are unphonetic. In these cases, you're not at fault at all. The words are spelled differently from the way they sound. With such unphonetic words, you're working without a net. There are no rules to lead you through this thicket. With unphonetic words, only spelling techniques like memorization and visualization can help you spell the words correctly.

The following study procedure can help you learn how to spell difficult words, such as unphonetic ones:

1. Pronounce the word. Use it in a sentence.
2. Visualize the word, syllable by syllable. Say the letters in order.
3. Close your eyes and spell the word. Check your answer.
4. Write the word. Check your answer.
5. Write the word five to ten times.

Unphonetic words fall into several categories, including *tricky word endings*, *y/i use*, and *unstressed vowels*. Let's start with confusing word endings.

TRICKY WORD ENDINGS

The following words confound even the best spellers because the words don't end the way we think they should:

1. Words that end in *ar* (but sound like they should end in *er*):

beggar   burglar
bursar   calendar
cellar   liar

2. Words that end in *ain* (but sound like they should end in *in*):

Britain   captain
certain   chieftain
curtain   mountain
porcelain   villain

> ALPHABETIC WRITING
> IS BASICALLY
> PHONETIC, BUT NO
> ALPHABET HAS EVER
> PERFECTLY
> REPRESENTED A
> LANGUAGE.

3. Words that end in *-cian* (but sound like they should end in *-tion*). Fortunately, there's help for this one, even though it's not based on the word's sound. End the word with *-cian* (rather than *-tion*) if you can trace it back to a word that ends in *-ic*. Here are some examples:

-Ic Word	-Cian Word
electric	electrician
music	musician
logic	logician
pediatric	pediatrician
politic	politician
mathematics	mathematician
optic	optician
pediatric	pediatrician
statistic	statistician

HOOKED ON PHONETICS WERKED FUR ME

Select the misspelled word in each group. Wait, you're not done yet! Then spell the word correctly on the line provided. Pretty please?

1. mathematician   pediatrician   electrictiono

_____

2. burglar   begger   bursar

_____

3. villain	captin	Britain
4. musician	optiction	logician
5. Britain	certain	porcelin
6. celler	villain	seminar
7. liar	calender	samovar
8. pediatrician	statistician	politition
9. burser	Zanzibar	kitchen
10. mountain	chieftin	curtain

ANSWERS

1. electrician	6. cellar
2. beggar	7. calendar
3. captain	8. politician
4. optician	9. bursar
5. porcelain	10. chieftain

FROM THE FRYING PAN TO THE FIRE: MORE UNPHONETIC WORDS

A speller's work is never done! Here's a posse of unphonetic words that you'll find useful in everyday life, especially if they're spelled correctly!

1. Either y or i. The words below sound like they contain an *i*. No such luck; each has a *y* that creates the *i* sound.

abyss	analyze	anonymous
cylinder	cynical	hypocrisy
paralysis	syllable	symmetry
sympathy	symphony	synonym
synthesis	tyranny	

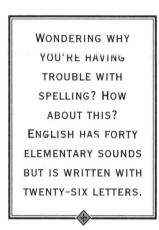

2. When it's *e*, not *i*. Sometimes life is unfair because you expect one thing but get another. Unfortunately, language can work the same way: you expect one letter but you get another. *E* and *i* are cases in point. Unphonetic sounds like these can make a speller's task all the more difficult.

Help is on the way. Study this list of unphonetic words. All contain an *e* where you would expect an *i*.

beauteous	courteous	delineate
erroneous	extemporaneous	hideous
liquefy	malleable	meteor
nauseate	piteous	simultaneous
spontaneous		

3. Unstressed vowel sounds. Perhaps the trickiest words in English are those that contain unstressed, or lightly stressed, vowels. These words account for a vast number of common spelling errors. Many vowels, ready for their close-ups in unstressed syllables, minimally lose their unique character and are correctly pronounced as a vague sound. There's actually a name for this sound, the *schwa*. It's written like this: ə. Check the pronunciation chart for more on the *schwa*.

Consider, for example, the middle syllable of the words *definite* and *separate*. One is spelled with an *i*, the other with an *a*, yet both are pronounced the same: *uh*. In this instance, since both *i* and *a* have the same *uh* sound, how can you choose the correct letter when you spell the words? Here are some suggestions:

1. Learn the most commonly misspelled unphonetic words.
2. Pronounce the unstressed vowel in an exaggerated way until you have learned the spelling.
3. Write the word several times until you have it down pat.

Here are some special offenders:

Word	Unstressed Letter
benefit	e (1st)
calendar	a (2nd)
definite	i (1st)
despair	e
dollar	a
existence	e (2nd)
origin	i (1st)
privilege	i (2nd)
sponsor	o (1st)

You can often figure out the correct vowel in an unstressed syllable by thinking of a closely related word in which the vowel is stressed, and therefore heard clearly. Fortunately, there's a huge list of these words, so all is not lost. Here are some words to get you started:

Vowel	Unclear (Unstressed Syllable)	Clear (Stressed Syllable)
e	arithmetic	arithmetical
e (2nd)	celebrate	celebrity
e (2nd)	competition	compete
o (1st)	frivolous	frivolity
i	hypocrisy	hypocritical
a (2nd)	narrative	narrate
o	revolution	revolt
a	sedative	sedate

THE UNPHONETIC SPELLINGS IN ENGLISH—SUCH AS **REIGN** AND **LIGHT**—HAVE INSPIRED MANY ATTEMPTS AT SPELLING REFORM. THE LAST MAJOR ATTEMPT AT SPELLING REFORM, AROUND 1900, RESULTED IN AT LEAST TWO REAL CHANGES: **MUSIC** FOR **MUSICK** AND **CATALOG** FOR **CATALOGUE**.

PHUN WITH PHONETICS

Below is a list of ten misspelled words. Each is unphonetic. Correct the spelling of each word and explain why the word is unphonetic. (And no fair saying that it's cranky, nasty, or out to get you.)

Word	Reason for Confusion
1. sillable	
2. dispair	
3. irroneous	
4. existance	
5. analize	
6. dollr	
7. Meditirranean	
8. orgin	
9. hipocrisy	
10. liquify	

ANSWERS

Word	Reason for Confusion
1. syllable	y creates the i sound
2. despair	unstressed vowel
3. erroneous	contains an e where you expect an i
4. existence	unstressed vowel
5. analyze	y creates the i sound
6. dollar	unstressed vowel
7. Mediterranean	contains an e where you expect an i
8. origin	unstressed vowel
9. hypocrisy	y creates the i sound
10. liquefy	contains an e where you expect an i

UNPHONETIC FENDER BENDERS

The following unphonetic words don't fit into any clear-cut categories. Rather, they exist solely to drive us crazy. To prevent further unnecessary mental anguish, here, then, are twenty-five useful and important unphonetic words:

biscuit	bouquet
brooch	buoy
bureau	chamois
colonel	Connecticut
draught	forfeit
furlough	hiccough
lieutenant	naive
parliament	pigeon
quay	sergeant
sieve	sovereign
suite	surgeon
ukulele	Wednesday
yacht	

Bonus: (one to drive you over the edge): naphtha.

> WE CAN TRACE MANY DIFFERENCES BETWEEN BRITISH AND AMERICAN SPELLINGS, SUCH AS THE AMERICAN **LABOR** FOR THE BRITISH **LABOUR**, TO NOAH WEBSTER.

RUMBLE IN THE JUNGLE

Match each word to its correct spelling. Place the letter of the correct spelling in the space provided.

_____1. yach	a. lieutenant
_____2. shammy	b. pigeon
_____3. ukelaylee	c. parliament
_____4. pigon	d. sovereign
_____5. furlow	e. yacht
_____6. kernol	f. sergeant
_____7. Connecut	g. naive
_____8. parlament	h. colonel
_____9. forfit	i. ukulele
_____10. sergant	j. forfeit

_____11. burow   k. chamois
_____12. lootenant   l. furlough
_____13. nieve   m. bureau
_____14. soverearn   n. Connecticut

PLAYING FAVORITES

We all have our favorite unphonetic words, the ones that drive us 'round the bend. But I could make a good case that the sound *sh* is the most annoying of all. Why? Well, *sh* can be formed in at least twenty-four different ways. Here are a few examples:

Sh Sound	Word
sh as *s*	sugar
sh as *sch*	schwa
sh as *se*	nauseous
sh as *si*	mansion
sh as *ss*	assure
sh as *ssh*	Bysshe (the poet Shelley)
sh as *ssi*	mission
sh as *c*	appreciate
sh as *ce*	ocean
sh as *ch*	chaperone
sh as *che*	cache
sh as *chsi*	fuchsia
sh as *ci*	suspicion
sh as *psh*	pshaw
sh as *esc*	crescendo
sh as *ti*	nation

And let us not forget *sh* as in *sh*. How about *shoe?*

THERE ARE EVEN MORE PHONETIC VARIATIONS IF WE CONSIDER PROPER NOUNS—THE NAMES OF PEOPLE AND PLACES.

CHAPTER 8

$\mathscr{L}$OOSE LIPS SINK SHIPS

YOU MUST REMEMBER THIS
We often misspell words because we mispronounce
them. Here are the big three mistakes:

1. We drop a letter or syllable when we say
   a word.
2. We insert an unnecessary letter when we
   say a word.
3. We mispronounce a word and so misspell
   it.

ALL THE RIGHT MOVES
Learn how to use a pronunciation key. Then check a
dictionary to make sure you've got the right sounds to
match each letter.

A few extra letters can have big consequences. For example, take the famous story of President John F. Kennedy's visit to Berlin in the early 1960s. Wishing to honor the Germans by speaking a bit of the language, Kennedy and his speech writers decided on the simple phrase: "I am a Berliner." Unfortunately, someone did a word-for-word literal translation: *Ich bin ein Berliner*. The appropriate phrase is *Ich bin Berliner*. Leave out that *ein*, please. What did Kennedy really say? "I am a jelly donut." Ouch.

One of the easiest, most effective ways to become a super speller is to pronounce words correctly, getting every one of those itty-bitty letters correct. As you learned in the previous chapter, English has a number of words, like *rhyme* and *reason*, that are spelled differently from the way they sound. Despite these exceptions, however, knowing the correct pronunciation for a word can often help you eliminate many spelling errors—and prevent some of those embarrassing jelly-donut incidents.

LOST AND FOUND

Let's start with words that are frequently misspelled because writers can't hold on to all their letters.

Here are ten words that are frequently misspelled because the speaker drops a letter or syllable.

> HOW DO YOU PRONOUNCE THE WORD **WAISTCOAT**? SOME PEOPLE SAY **WES**-KUT, WHILE OTHERS PREFER **WAYST**-KOTE.

1. accidentally *Accidentally* has five syllables; drop one and you'll most likely lose the *al*. As a result, our *accidentally* becomes *accidently*. Remember that this word has five syllables so poor "Al" doesn't get lost in the shuffle.

2. accompaniment The second *a* and the only *i* are the problems with accompaniment. Some inventive spellers have even been known to substitute a *y* for the *i*. Consider yourself forewarned. To remember the *i*, you might want to use this mnemonic: there's a lot of *animal* in *accompaniment*.

3. acreage The *e* presents the spelling problem because it is rarely stressed in speech. That's how people end up with *acrage*. It's also not uncommon for writers to remember the *e* at the last minute, but place it in the wrong place, as in *acerage*. No missing *e*'s or last-minute ones when you write *acreage*!

4. anecdote Many letters get dropped when writers mispronounce *anecdote* as *anedote*. Then there's *antidote*. Don't feel so bad if you've committed the latter spelling sin; it's an understandable error, since *antidote* is a legitimate word.

5. asked As a Long Islander (that slender spit of land in New York often called "Lawn Guyland" by its residents), I'm well used to *asked* getting mangled as *ast* or even *axed*. This results in such curious spellings as *askd, askt,* and *axst.* (Hey, so we don't talk so good on Lawn Guyland. At least we have some nice beaches.)

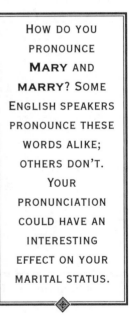

IN ENGLAND, THE WORD **HAPPSBURGH** IS PRONOUNCED **HEZ-BRUH.**

6. asterisk This handy but often mispronounced word can end up being spelled *aterisk, aksterisk,* or even *acksterisk.* If you're really in doubt and there's no dictionary handy, you can always use the symbol: *.

7. broccoli It's not hard to drop a *c* and add an *l* with this delicious, healthful, but sorely maligned veggie. The correct pronunciation isn't going to do you much good here, so try breaking the word into two parts: *broc* and *coli.* (And eat your spinach, too.)

HOW DO YOU PRONOUNCE **MARY** AND **MARRY**? SOME ENGLISH SPEAKERS PRONOUNCE THESE WORDS ALIKE; OTHERS DON'T. YOUR PRONUNCIATION COULD HAVE AN INTERESTING EFFECT ON YOUR MARITAL STATUS.

8. calisthenics Stress the first *i* and the *e* to avoid dropping these letters when you exercise your brain to spell *calisthenics.* Otherwise, you could end up with *calesthenics, calesthinics,* and a sore brain.

9. category The misspelled *catagory* results from a small shift in pronunciation. Make sure you say that *e* as an *e* rather than an *a* to avoid this spelling faux pas.

10. cemetery *Cemetary* is the result when the third *e* is pronounced as an *a.*

TEA TIME

To see how well you're doing so far, spell each of the following words correctly. Then write your responses on the lines provided. Note which letter was either silent or mispronounced.

Word	Correct Spelling	Letter(s)
1. calsthnics		
2. askd		
3. brocoli		
4. aterisk		
5. cemetary		
6. catagory		
7. accidently		
8. acrage		
9. anedote		
10. accompanyment		

ANSWERS

Correct Spelling	Letter
1. calisthenics	i, e
2. asked	e
3. broccoli	c
4. asterisk	s
5. cemetery	e
6. category	e
7. accidentally	al
8. acreage	e
9. anecdote	e
10. accompaniment	i

ACCORDING TO **RIPLEY'S BELIEVE IT OR NOT,** ONLY ONE
PERSON IN 100,000 CAN PRONOUNCE EVERY ONE OF THE
FOLLOWING TEN WORDS CORRECTLY. YOU HAVE JUST LEARNED HOW
IMPORTANT CORRECT PRONUNCIATION IS TO CORRECT SPELLING. HOW
WELL DO YOU MEASURE UP? GIVE IT A SHOT. THEN CHECK YOUR
PRONUNCIATIONS IN A DICTIONARY. HERE ARE THE WORDS:
**DATA, GRATIS, CULINARY, NUCLEAR, GONDOLA,
VERSION, IMPIOUS, CHIC, CARIBBEAN, VIKING.**
NOW, CAN YOU SPELL THEM AS WELL?

TAKE A LETTER, MARIA

You're not done yet! Here are ten more words that are often mangled because writers lose a letter somewhere along the line.

1. characteristic Again, we have five syllables— quite a mouthful. Lose one of the syllables and you've lost a letter or two, resulting in *charactristic* or *charcteristic*, to identify just two of the usual suspects.

HOW DO YOU PRONOUNCE **SOPHOMORE**? SOME PEOPLE SAY **SOF**-MORE; OTHERS, **SOF**-O-MORE.

2. chocolate Nature's most perfect food! Unfortunately, that *o* often vanishes as we cry out for *choclate*. Next time you reach for this delectable food, remember to include the *o* for extra taste.

3. disassemble *Dissemble* results when the *as* gets dropped. Now, this happens to be a word as well, just not the one the writer happens to want in this particular circumstance.

4. environment Many times, the second *n* gets lost in space, leaving us with these misspellings: *envirment* or *enviroment*.

5. government An extremely common mistake is to not pronounce the *n*, and so misspell the word as *goverment*.

6. grammar This word is often mangled as *grammer*, resulting in the obvious misspelling. Stress that *a* and you'll be A-OK.

DID YOU KNOW THAT THE **P** IN **PSYCHOLOGY** AND THE **K** IN **KNIFE** USED TO BE PRONOUNCED? OVER THE YEARS, THE PRONUNCIATION OF THESE WORDS CHANGED, BUT THE OLD PRONUNCIATION IS REFLECTED IN THEIR SPELLING. JUST OUR LUCK.

7. incidentally Again, we're juggling a whole lot of syllables—five, to be precise. Often, the *al* gets lost and so the word is misspelled as *incidently*.

8. laboratory Many times, the *o* is omitted, and our *laboratory* becomes *labratory*.

9. library Say that first *r* or you could end up writing *libary* or even *liberry*. Ouch; they could yank a library card for that.

10. outrageous The *e* gets dropped, resulting in *outragous*. The pronunciation isn't clear enough to really prevent this mistake, so remember to add just a hint of an *e* to spell it correctly.

MISSION POSSIBLE

I know you're right on target, but you may not realize how well you're doing. Reassure yourself by completing the following quiz. Circle the misspelled word in each word group below:

1. outrageous	outragous	acreage
2. enviroment	cemetery	environment
3. grammer	asked	grammar
4. incidently	accidentally	incidentally
5. choclate	calisthenics	chocolate
6. labratory	laboratory	accompaniment
7. characteristic	charactristic	asterisk
8. liberry	library	anecdote
9. goverment	government	broccoli
10. disassemble	disemble	category

ANSWERS

1. outrageous	6. laboratory
2. environment	7. characteristic
3. grammar	8. library
4. incidentally	9. government
5. chocolate	10. disassemble

YOU SAY TO-MAY-TO AND I SAY TOE-MAH-TO

Obviously, mispronunciation is a big spelling problem. Conquer it by learning how to correctly say and spell the following ten words. As with the preceding twenty words, these devilish words are frequently misspelled because speakers omit letters when they say them.

1. plaintiff The word is often pronounced *plainiff*, resulting in a lost *t*. To help you remember to include the *t* in *plaintiff*, try this mnemonic: a *plaintiff* starts a *tiff*.

2. quantity Like plaintiff, the first *t* is often omitted when people mispronounce *quantity* as *quanity*.

3. representative Due to sloppy speech, this word emerges as *represenative*, with the loss of a *t*.

4. sacrilegious Although this isn't a common word, it comes in for its fair share of verbal mangling. This results in such inventive variations as *sacriligious* and *sacreligious*.

5. separate When used as an adjective, this word is often mispronounced as *seperate*.

6. temperament *Temperament* is often mispronounced as *temperment*. Ironically, saying the word correctly can also lead to errors in spelling, such as *tempreament* and *temprament*.

7. temperature This word gets destroyed in two ways. First, it's often reduced to three syllables, resulting in *temperture*. Second, the *a* is lost in the shuffle, reinforcing the error. You can avoid this problem by saying all four syllables and slightly stressing the *a*.

THE QUESTION OF PRONUNCIATION IS ESPECIALLY ACUTE WITH PLACE NAMES. HOW DO YOU PRONOUNCE THESE PLACES: **GREENWICH**, **LEICESTER**, **HOUSTON**, AND **WARWICK?**

8. treacherous   *Treacherous* doesn't really belong on this list, because pronouncing it *correctly* leaves out the *a*, resulting in *trecherous*. I included the word anyway because it is so often used—and abused.

9. valuable That second *a* gets lost unless you remember to stress it when you say the word. Say the *a* to avoid spelling *valuable* as *valuble*.

10. Wednesday *Wensday* is the most common misspelling. Unfortunately, you can't put too much stress on that *d* or the word will sound weird. How about giving that *d* a little mental tweak to help you remember to include it?

SEVENTH INNING STRETCH

Take a stretch by completing this easy quiz. In each of the following groups of words, only one word is misspelled. Select the misspelled word and spell it correctly in the space provided. Pronounce each word carefully to make sure that you're including all the letters.

_____	1. represenative	outrageous
	representative	calisthenics
_____	2. broccoli	seperate
	similar	separate
_____	3. temperture	cemetery
	temperature	asterisk
_____	4. valuble	valuable
	disassemble	laboratory
_____	5. trecherous	treacherous
	accidentally	asked
_____	6. quanity	quantity
	environment	grammar
_____	7. plainiff	plaintiff
	incidentally	category

_____	8. Wenesday Wednesday
	chocolate acreage
_____	9. temperment temperament
	library government
_____	10. sacralegious quantity
	sacrilegious characteristic

ANSWERS

1. representative	6. quantity
2. separate	7. plaintiff
3. temperature	8. Wednesday
4. valuable	9. temperament
5. treacherous	10. sacrilegious

IN THIS CASE, LESS IS MORE!

Because of errors in pronunciation, spellers often insert an unnecessary vowel between two letters. Here are some of the most common boo-boos:

1. **athlete** *Athlete* is often mispronounced as *athalete*, resulting in that unnecessary *a*.

2. **disastrous** When said incorrectly, *disastrous* ends up with *disaster* stuck in there: *disasterous*. What extra letter do you see?

3. **grievous** Another common speech slip results in *grieveous* or *grievious*. No extra *e* or *i*, please.

4. **hindrance** *Hindrance* falls prey to the same problem as *disastrous*: add *hinder* to *hindrance* and you get *hinderance*. Too many syllables!

5. **lightning** You met this electrifying word in Chapter 1, when I mentioned how mispronunciations often result in misspellings. The bolt of electricity on a stormy night is often mispronounced and thus misspelled as *lightening*. Now, *lightening* is a legitimate

word; it means that something is getting less dark. Saying each word correctly will help you correctly spell the one you really want.

> HOW DO YOU PRONOUNCE THE WORD **DOUR**? IS IT **DOOR** OR **DOWER**? CHECK YOUR DICTIONARY TO SEE WHAT IT SAYS.

6. mischievous A surprising number of people mispronounce the word as *mischievious*, adding that extra *i*. Drop the unnecessary second *i* and you're home free with this tricky spelling word.

7. perseverance People often add an extra *r*, resulting in *perserverance*. Saying the word correctly will prevent this error.

TAKE A BREAK

You deserve a break today. Take one by writing the spelling word that matches each definition. Use the words you just learned.

Definition	Spelling Word
1. determination	
2. obstacle	
3. calamitous	
4. to make lighter	
5. full of mischief	
6. sportsperson	
7. lamentable	
8. bolt of electricity	

ANSWERS

1. perseverance
2. hindrance
3. disastrous
4. lightening

5. mischievous
6. athlete
7. grievous
8. lightning

SCRAMBLED LETTERS

Mispronunciation can also result in scrambled letters. In our defense, many of these scrambled words are killers to pronounce in the first place. Nonetheless, such spelling errors can sometimes even make it impossible to figure out what the word is. The following chart shows some of the most commonly scrambled words.

Most Commonly Garbled Words

Word	Scramblings
aesthetic	aeshetic
allegiance	alligeance
analysis	analsyis
analyze	anylaze
anonymous	anyonmous
antecedent	anteceednt
auxiliary	auxilairy
bureaucracy	buracueracy
diaphragm	diagphram
entrepreneur	enterpreneur
gasoline	gasolene
gauge	guage
gorgeous	gorgoeus
irrelevant	irrelavent
khaki	kahki
languorous	langourous
lingerie	lingiree
mileage	milage

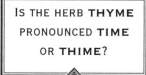

IS THE HERB **THYME** PRONOUNCED **TIME** OR **THIME?**

LONGTIME SPEAKERS AND READERS OF ENGLISH HAVE LEARNED BASIC CONNECTIONS BETWEEN SOUNDS AND LETTER COMBINATIONS THAT HELP THEM SPELL A LARGE NUMBER OF WORDS. HOWEVER, FOR HISTORICAL REASONS, CERTAIN COMBINATIONS OF LETTERS ARE NOT ALWAYS PRONOUNCED IN THE SAME WAY. FOR EXAMPLE, **OUGH** CAN BE PRONOUNCED DIFFERENTLY, AS IN **THOUGHT, BOUGH, THROUGH, DROUGHT.**

obsequious	obsiqueous
psychology	pyschology
reconnaissance	reconaissannce
resuscitate	resucsitate
rhyme	ryhme
rhythm	ryhthm

UNSCRAMBLE THESE!

Unscramble these often garbled words by matching each word to its correct spelling. Draw lines between each scrambled word and its correct spelling.

Scrambled Words	Correct Spellings
1. haraunge	perspiration
2. hieght	syringe
3. hemohrroid	sergeant
4. hienous	perverse
5. hemorrahge	sapphire
6. heirarchy	paradigm
7. horses d'ovaries	yield
8. paradimg	pharaoh
9. prespiration	hemorrhoid
10. preverse	weight
11. pharoah	hierarchy
12. peom	harangue
13. saphpire	tragedy
14. sargent	hemorrhage
15. syrnige	heinous
16. tradgey	hors d'oeuvre
17. wieght	poem
18. yeild	height

ANSWERS

Scrambled Words	Correct Spellings
1. haraunge	harangue
2. hieght	height
3. hemohrroid	hemorrhoid
4. hienous	heinous
5. hemorrahge	hemorrhage
6. heirarchy	hierarchy
7. horses d'ovaries	hors d'oeuvres
8. paradimg	paradigm
9. prespiration	perspiration
10. preverse	perverse
11. pharoah	pharaoh
12. peom	poem
13. saphpire	sapphire
14. sargent	sergeant
15. syrnige	syringe
16. tradgey	tragedy
17. wieght	weight
18. yeild	yield

CHAPTER 9

BROTHER, CAN YOU SPARE

A WORD OR TWO?

YOU MUST REMEMBER THIS
Judging from the number of words English has imported from other countries, it's plain that we don't subscribe to the maxim "Neither a borrower nor a lender be."

ALL THE RIGHT MOVES
A word's origins often determine how it is spelled. Look for patterns among words with common linguistic roots.

"Give me your tired, your poor, your huddled masses yearning to breathe free," read the words from a sonnet by Emma Lazarus inscribed on the pedestal of the Statue of Liberty. She was probably thinking more of sheltering people than she was of words, but with one came the other.

English is the most democratic and unrestricted language that has ever existed. We have welcomed into our vocabulary words from scores of other languages and dialects, near and far, ancient and modern. The problem? Now we have to learn to spell all these words—and they rarely fit the English spelling rules.

Fortunately, it's a lot easier than you might think, and the reward is worth it: a rich, expressive vocabulary. Here are three hints to get you started spelling non-English-based words:

1. Note the foreign roots for words you have difficulty spelling. You can find this information in the dictionary, right after the word itself.
2. Try to link the root to other related words you need to

spell. For example, the Latin root *circum-* (around) can help you figure out how to spell such words as *circumvent* and *circumscribe*.

3. Even if you can't use the root to help you spell the word now, try to use it to create a mnemonic that can help you remember how to spell the word next time.

In this chapter, we'll explore some of the words that have entered English from other languages and the special spelling problems those words present.

DUTY FREE: IMPORTED WORDS

English never rejects a word because of race, creed, or national origin. Let me prove it to you. Take this simple quiz to match each of the following words with its native language. Write the letter of the correct choice in the blank by the number.

Word	Origin
Word	**Origin**
____1. kimono	a. Arabic
____2. tomato	b. West Indian
____3. camel	c. Senegalese
____4. algebra	d. Malayan
____5. typhoon	e. Japanese
____6. yam	f. French
____7. mahogany	g. Mexican
____8. ketchup	h. Yiddish
____9. klutz	i. Hebrew
____9. klutz	i. Hebrew
____9. klutz	i. Hebrew
____10. aspic	j. Chinese

ANSWERS

1. e	6. c
2. g	7. b
3. i	8. d
4. a	9. h
5. j	10. f

FROM FRENCH WE BORROWED THE WORD **COUP**, WHICH MEANS "TO STRIKE A BLOW." A **COUP D'ETAT** IS THE VIOLENT OVERTHROW OF A GOVERNMENT; A **COUP DE GRACE** IS A DEATH BLOW. A **COUP DE MAIN** IS A FORCEFUL ATTACK; A **COUP DE THEATRE**, A GREAT THEATRICAL SUCCESS.

So where did we get all the words that enable you to express yourself precisely in speech and writing? Many of them traveled to English in ships and steerage, on the *QE2* and the *Mayflower*. Let's survey some of the richest sources of our words, the countries of England, France, Spain, Italy, Germany, Poland, and Ireland. Then we'll discuss some words from the Arab states, India, and Iran.

Let's look at some specific words that entered English from our neighbors around the globe. We'll start with our neighbors across the pond—the British.

BRITISH CONTRIBUTIONS

To American eyes, some British spellings look like they should be yanked. But after all, the folks on the other side of the pond *did* start the language, so we have to show a little respect—even though we vastly improved the language. Nearly all the differences are found in word endings, especially suffixes. Here's your basic cheat sheet:

British Spelling	American Spelling
-our (colour)	*-or* (color)
-ement (judgement)	*-ment* (judgment)
-xion (connexion)	*-tion* (connection)
-ise (criticise)	*-ize* (criticize)
-re (centre)	*-er* (center)
-lled (travelled)	*-led* (traveled)

OTHER AMERICAN/BRITISH VARIATIONS INCLUDE **GRAY/GREY** AND **CHECK/CHEQUE.**

I SPY

Take the following quiz to see if you could pass as a British spy in the United States . . . or would your spelling betray you? Write the American spelling for each of the following words:

British	American
1. aeon	
2. haemorrhage	
3. kerb	
4. carburettor	

5. speciality

6. waggon

7. artefact

8. connexion

9. apologise

10. enrol

11. cyder

12. to-morrrow

13. gaol

14. dulness

15. syphon

16. pyjamas

17. nought

18. vice

19. pretence

20. anaemic

21. harbour

22. biassed

23. mediaeval

24. worshipper

25. behove

ANSWERS

American

1. eon	9. apologize	17. naught
2. hemorrhage	10. enroll	18. vise
3. curb	11. cider	19. pretense
4. carburetor	12. tomorrow	20. anemic
5. specialty	13. jail	21. harbor
6. wagon	14. dullness	22. biased
7. artifact	15. siphon	23. medieval
8. connection	16. pajamas	24. worshiper
		25. behoove

PARLEZ-VOUS ANGLAIS? ENGLISH WORDS FROM FRENCH

The French have given us some tasty bread, fine wine, stylish clothing—and some useful but challenging spelling words. Here are fifteen of the most often encountered spelling demons from French and their definitions:

Word	Definition
au contraire	on the contrary
à votre santé	to your health
bête noire	black beast; someone or something greatly disliked
bon appétit	good appetite
bonjour	good day; hello
carte blanche	blank check; complete power to act a certain way
c'est la vie	that's life
esprit de corps	group spirit
laissez-faire	hands-off policy
noblesse oblige	responsibility of high rank
pied-à-terre	second home
raison d'être	reason for being
salle à manger	dining room
s'il vous plaît	please
soup du jour	soup of the day

Here are twenty more words that have entered English from French. On the following chart, underline each word from French that you find especially hard to spell.

Word	Meaning
bon mot	clever saying
bon vivant	person who lives well
bourgeois	middle class
charlatan	faker, quack
ennui	boredom
faux pas	social blunder
gauche	socially inept
genteel	elegant, refined
harangue	vehement speech
hauteur	arrogance
idee fixe	obsession

WE ADOPTED THE FRENCH PHRASE **VIVE LA DIFFERENCE** ("LONG LIVE THE DIFFERENCE") TO DESCRIBE THE PLEASANT AS WELL AS BAFFLING DIFFERENCES BETWEEN MEN AND WOMEN.

insouciance	carefree
largesse	generosity
malaprop	misused word
nonchalance	indifference
poseur	affected manner
rapport	harmony, accord
repartee	witty talk
raconteur	expert storyteller
sang-froid	cool under pressure

ARMCHAIR TRAVELER

Imagine sitting in a small bistro in the shadow of the Arc d' Triomphe, nibbling a rich brie and sipping an iced coffee. Ah, heaven on earth! To prepare for your trip, correct the spelling of each of the following English words from French.

Word	Correct Spelling
1. inssouciance	
2. laisez-faire	
3. charletan	
4. noblese oblige	
5. harrangue	
6. raconture	
7. bon appetite	
8. bourgois	
9. gentele	
10. cart blanche	

LATIN GAVE US MANY IMPORTANT WORDS THAT CAN PRESENT
SPELLING DIFFICULTIES. HERE ARE FOUR KEY TERMS: **AD HOC**
(IMPROVISED), **AD NAUSEAM** (TO A SICKENING DEGREE),
CAVEAT EMPTOR (LET THE BUYER BEWARE), AND
STATUS QUO (THE EXISTING SITUATION).

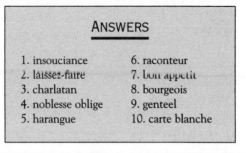

ANSWERS

1. insouciance	6. raconteur
2. laissez-faire	7. bon appetit
3. charlatan	8. bourgeois
4. noblesse oblige	9. genteel
5. harangue	10. carte blanche

ENGLISH WORDS FROM SPANISH

Up until the sixteenth century, English was only lightly flavored with Spanish. Queen Mary's marriage to Philip II of Spain changed all that. Even though "Bloody Mary's" reign lasted only five years before her half-sister Queen Elizabeth took charge, it was enough time to forge a strong link between

IN SPANISH, **AMARILLO** MEANS "YELLOW."

the English and Spanish courts. Spanish coins, articles of trade, and words were all freely exchanged. Now, four hundred years later, the money and spices are musty relics, but nearly all the words remain fresh and useful.

Below are fifteen useful words that entered English from Spanish. Each of these words stumps many spellers. Match each word to its correct spelling. Write the letter of the correct spelling in the space provided.

	Misspelled	**Correct**
_____	1. barbacue	a. adobe
_____	2. maranade	b. anchovy
_____	3. pimentoe	c. arroyo
_____	4. patioe	d. avocado
_____	5. seirra	e. barbecue
_____	6. aroyo	f. canyon
_____	7. sasparala	g. hacienda
_____	8. vanila	h. marinade
_____	9. anchovie	i. patio
_____	10. torteea	j. pimento
_____	11. hacenda	k. sierra
_____	12. avacado	l. sarsaparilla
_____	13. adobbe	m. tortilla
_____	14. canyun	n. vanilla

ANSWERS

1. e	6. c	11. g
2. h	7. l	12. d
3. j	8. n	13. a
4. i	9. b	14. f
5. k	10. m	

ENGLISH WORDS FROM ITALIAN

Many of our imported Italian words are in art, music, and literature, but other areas have been flavored by Italian as well. How many of these born-in-Italy words can you spell? Write C if the spelling is correct; write X if it is wrong.

_____ 1. bravo
_____ 2. impresario
_____ 3. allegro
_____ 4. bandit
_____ 5. barrack
_____ 6. citadel
_____ 7. fracas
_____ 8. vendetta
_____ 9. maestro
_____ 10. legato

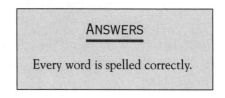

ANSWERS

Every word is spelled correctly.

ENGLISH WORDS FROM YIDDISH

The speed with which Yiddish words and phrases have entered English is dazzling. Leo Rosten, the late expert on Yiddish, once commented that a person could not spend a day in any major American or British city without hearing a cluster of words gathered from Yiddish.

See how many of these Jewish-American foods you can spell. Circle the correct spelling in each word group.

1. blintzes   blintes   blines
2. borsht   borscht   barscht
3. chalah   callah   challah
4. gefalte fish gefilte fish gefile fish
5. knaydl   knadl   naydl
6. nish   knish   knishe
7. replach   kreplach   kreppllach
8. loxe   loch   lox
9. mazoth   metzoth   matzo

ANSWERS

1. blintzes   6. knish
2. borscht   7. kreplach
3. challah   8. lox
4. gefilte fish 9. matzo
5. knaydl

ENGLISH WORDS FROM IRISH (CELTIC)

Here are some words that have come into English from our Irish immigrants. In the space provided, write **T** if the word is spelled correctly or **F** if it is misspelled.

_____1. graval
_____2. lawn
_____3. truant
_____4. shamrock
_____5. vasal
_____6. galore
_____7. banshie
_____8. plaid
_____9. colleen
_____10. wiskey

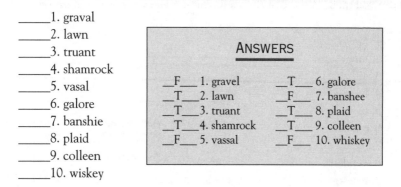

ANSWERS

_F__ 1. gravel   _T__ 6. galore
_T__ 2. lawn   _F__ 7. banshee
_T__ 3. truant   _T__ 8. plaid
_T__ 4. shamrock   _T__ 9. colleen
_F__ 5. vassal   _F__ 10. whiskey

ENGLISH WORDS FROM THE ARAB STATES, INDIA, AND IRAN

The Arab states, India, and Iran have also made significant contributions to English. Arabic contributed the most words, usually filtered through French or Spanish. The majority of these words entered English as a result of trading.

Draw a line to match each word with its correct spelling.

1. nabbob
2. alcemy
3. nervana
4. gooroo
5. areil
6. albecore
7. taragon
8. punditt
9. safron
10. hena
11. nadeer
12. kamra
13. bannadana
14. garbble
15. campor

saffron
garble
tarragon
camphor
nabob
bandanna
alchemy
karma
nirvana
albacore
guru
nadir
pundit
ariel
henna

> WITH PRACTICE, YOU'LL DISCOVER CERTAIN BASIC PATTERNS THAT LINK SPELLING TO WORD SOUNDS.

ANSWERS

1. nabob	9. saffron
2. alchemy	10. henna
3. nirvana	11. nadir
4. guru	12. karma
5. ariel	13. bandanna
6. albacore	14. garble
7. tarragon	15. camphor
8. pundit	

HERE ARE SOME OTHER USEFUL WORDS FROM ARABIC AND INDIAN LANGUAGES THAT CAN BE HARD TO SPELL: **ALGORITHM, ELIXIR, CIPHER, ALKALI, MONSOON, CARAFE, ZENITH, CALIBER, AVATAR.**

THE ACCENT'S ON SOMEWHERE

An *accent* is a mark of punctuation that affects the way a word is pronounced.

In addition to arranging the letters in the right places, now you have to worry about placing accents on the correct letters. Some accents go to the right, others go to the left. One accent points up like the roof on a house; another is two cute little dots. Don't get your stomach in knots; accent placement is much easier than it seems.

First of all, here's a run-down on the most common accents:

Name of Symbol	Symbol	Example
acute	´ (up from left to right) accent for vowels	résumé
grave	` (down from left to right) accent for vowels	crème de menthe

Name of Symbol	Symbol	Example
circumflex	^ accent for vowels	crêpe
umlaut	¨ (two dots) accent for vowels	München (Munich)
tilde	~ accent mark for the letter n	jalapeño

Second, relatively few words in English have accents. Here's where English gives you a break; French and Spanish are killers with those accents. In addition, knowing the accents is actually a plus, because it can help you say and thus spell a word correctly. Try it now.

Use what you already know and a dictionary to place the accents on each of the following words that have entered English from other languages.

Word	Language	Meaning	Word with Accents
1. manana	Spanish	tomorrow	
2. melee	French	riot	
3. pieta	Italian	Virgin Mary	
4. creche	French	Nativity	
5. detente	French	relaxation of tension	
6. deja vu	French	already experienced	
7. fuhrer	German	tyrant	
8. tete-a-tete	French	in private	
9. boite	French	nightclub	
10. emigre	French	emigrant	

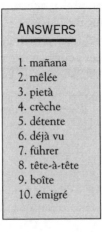

ANSWERS

1. mañana
2. mêlée
3. pietà
4. crèche
5. détente
6. déjà vu
7. führer
8. tête-à-tête
9. boîte
10. émigré

PART II:

$\mathscr{S}$PELLING WORDS

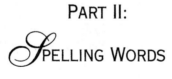

• • • •

Teddy Roosevelt was "surprized" at the ruckus "razed" in response to his 1906 order to the public printer. In it, he listed 300 words that henceforth would be spelled according to the Simplified Spelling Board guidelines.

Funded by the millionaire industrialist and philanthropist Andrew Carnegie, the organization crusaded for deleting the *u* in *honour* and *parlour*, changes that eventually came into general usage. However, more radical ideas, such as *kist* for *kissed* and *tho* for *though*, have not endured. And for this we do give thanks!

The press reacted to TR's order with scorn. One editor wrote that "nuting escapes Mr. Ruzevelt. No subject is tu tuff fr him to takl, nor tu lo for him tu notis."

Questioning the president's power to change American orthography, Congress instructed the printing office that all material sent to its chambers contain standard spelling.

In response to the general outcry, Roosevelt regretfully withdrew his order. Yet he later wrote that he was glad he "did the right thing anyhow." Some kids never learn.

CHAPTER 10:

*S*PELLING DEMONS

YOU MUST REMEMBER THIS
Spelling demons are the bad boys in the back of the class: they don't follow the rules.

ALL THE RIGHT MOVES
Since many of these words are important and used often, just bite the bullet and memorize them.

How can you tell a spelling demon? Here are three clues:

1. It's the word that looks wrong even when it's spelled correctly.
2. It's the word that makes even good spellers gnaw (or is that "naw"?) on their fingernails in frustration.

3. It's the word you have to spell on an important document when you don't have a dictionary to consult.

I know you can spell *all right* because it's the opposite of *all wrong*. Maybe you were lucky enough to learn that *a lot* is two words, *rarefy* has that pesky *e*, and *sacrilegious* has a whole lot of letters.

But there are still multitudes of words lying (laying?) in wait for you. Below is a list of spelling demons you're likely to encounter in daily life. The list includes the most commonly used—and abused—words. These words are most likely to be misspelled, and in some of the most interesting ways, too.

Of course, there are many more such difficult words, so don't write to me, e-mail me, or fax me your favorite killers. I've given you a few lines in the bottom of each category where you can record your favorite toughies.

A

abbreviate
abhor
abscess
absence
abundant
abyss
academic
accede
accelerate
accept
accessory
accommodate
accompany
accumulate
acetic (meaning: sour)
ache
achievement
acknowledge
acknowledging
acknowledgment
acquainted
acquiesce
acquire
across
addendum
address
adjacent
adjudicate
admissible
adolescence
adrenaline
adultery
adverse
adviser or advisor
aesthetic or esthetic
affect
aggravate
aggression

agriculture
aid
aide
aisle
Albuquerque
alleluia or hallelujah
allot
allotted
a lot
all ready
already
all right
allspice
allude
allusion
altar
alter
alumna
alumnus
always
amateur
amend
among
analyses (plural)
analysis (singular)
analyze
anchor
anecdote
annihilate
anniversary
annual
annul
anoint
antecedent
antidote
antique
antiseptic
aperitif

aperture
apostrophe
appall or appal
apparel
apparent
appetite
appraise
apprise
apropos
arrogant
ascertain
ancestry
anxiety
anywhere
apiece
ascetic
assess
asterisk
atheist
athlete
atrocity
attention
audible
au lait
au naturel
authentic
autumn
avalanche
averse
awesome
awry

My Favorite Spelling Demons That Start with A

_____

_____

_____

_____

_____

_____

So what's it going to be: **HAREBRAINED** or **HAIRBRAINED**? (The former, as in **HARELIP**.)

TEST YOURSELF

Match the incorrectly spelled word with its correctly spelled counterpart. Write the letter of the answer in the space provided.

_____1. athiest

_____2. audable

_____3. au naturale

_____4. awrye

_____5. abhorr

_____6. anihilate

_____7. stericke

_____8. aniversary

_____9. asess

_____10. abiss

_____11. alot

_____12. alspice

_____13. accross

_____14. awsome

_____15. acqueisce

_____16. aversse

_____17. acknowleging

_____18. ajudicate

_____19. acedemic

_____20. absense

a. academic

b. averse

c. allspice

d. anniversary

e. atheist

f. awesome

g. a lot

h. abhor

i. annihilate

j. abyss

k. adjudicate

l. across

m. audible

n. asterisk

o. assess

p. acquiesce

q. awry

r. acknowledging

s. absence

t. au naturel

To help prevent spelling and pronunciation misconceptions, try to visualize the word as you spell it.

ANSWERS

1. e	6. i	11. g	16. b
2. m	7. n	12. c	17. r
3. t	8. d	13. l	18. k
4. q	9. o	14. f	19. a
5. h	10. j	15. p	20. s

B

babushka
baccalaureate
bachelor
badminton
balalaika
balloon
banal
banana
baptism
baptize
barbecue
barrette
bathe
battalion
bazaar (a market)
beggar
beige
belligerent
bellwether
benefactor
benefited
belief
believed
benign
berserk
bialys
biannual
bicycle

biennial
bigamy
birthday
bizarre
boisterous
bologna
bona fide
bootie or bootee (baby shoe)
booty (plunder)
boudoir
bouillabaisse
bouillon (broth)
bourgeois
Braille
brassiere
breath (exhaled air)
breathe (to inhale)
brethren
Britain (country)
Briton (citizen of Britain)
broach (to open)
brooch (pin)
broccoli
bruise
brusque
buccaneer
bucolic
budget
buffet
bullion (gold)

bouillon (broth)
bureau
burglar
business
bylaw or by-law
byline
bypass
by-product
byte (computer symbol)
byword

My Favorite Spelling Demons That Start with B

_____

_____

_____

_____

_____

_____

JOHNNY B GOOD

Here's a little test to see how well you remember some bothersome "b" words. Next to each of the ten words below, provide the correct spelling. The answer box is right nearby, so you'll have to cover it with your hand while you quiz yourself. No peeking!

A FEW DICTIONARIES CLAIM THAT **BROCOLI** IS AN ACCEPTABLE SPELLING. HOWEVER, SINCE ALL THE WORDSMITHS HAVE YET TO FOLLOW SUIT, STICK WITH THE OLD RELIABLE **BROCCOLI.**

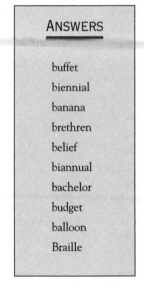

ANSWERS

Word		Answer
bufet	_____	buffet
beinnial	_____	biennial
bananana	_____	banana
bretren	_____	brethren
beleif	_____	belief
byannual	_____	biannual
bachalor	_____	bachelor
buget	_____	budget
baloon	_____	balloon
bralle	_____	Braille

C

cache (hiding place)
cachet (approval)
cafe au lait
cafeteria
caffeine
calendar
California
calisthenics
callous (hard)
callus (hard skin)
camaraderie
camouflage
campaign
candidate
cantaloupe *or* cantaloup
capital (assets)
capitol (building)
capsule
career
Caribbean
carnival
carol
carousel
carrel
carte blanche
cartilage
castanets
catalyst
catastrophe
category
cede
ceiling
celebrate
celebrity
celestial
cellophane
cemetery
cemeteries

censer
censor
censure
cerebral
chafe
chaise lounge
champagne
champaign
chandelier
chaos
chasm
chassis
chauffeur
chief
chicanery
chickle
chocolate
cholesterol
choose
chose
chosen
cigarette
circuit
circumstance
cirrhosis
cite
clandestine
claret
classify
cleanse
cliché
clique
coalesce
coarse
co-author
cocoa
codicil
coerce
coiffeur (hairdresser)
coiffure (hairstyle)

coincide
collaborate
colleague
colonel
column
comeback (witty reply)
come back (return)
commemorate
commensurate
committee
communicate
compel
complement
compliment
compos mentis
comprise
concede
conceited
conceive
concierge
conciliatory
concise
concoct
condemn
condescend
condominium
confidant *and*
  confidante
confident
conjugal
Connecticut
connoisseur
conscience
conscientious
conscious
consensus
consistent
constituent
constitute
consul

consummate
contemporary
contentious
contradict
convalesce
coordinate
corespondent (adulterer)
corollary
corporate
correspond
correspondent (writer)
corroborate
council
counsel
coup d'etat
courteous
create
credence
credible
credulity
crescendo
criteria (plural)
criterion (singular)
criticize
crowd
currant (raisin)
current (now; electricity)
curricula (singular)
curriculum (plural)
cylinder

My Favorite Spelling Demons That Start with C

_____

_____

_____

_____

_____

_____

C How You Do

There are twenty-five spelling words that begin with "c" hidden in the following puzzle. To complete the puzzle, locate and circle all the words. The words may be written forward or backward. Good luck!

Here are the words to look for:

chose	crescendo	carol
chandelier	chasm	constituent
cylinder	consul	committee
concoct	compel	catastrophe
coincide	cite	cache
create	claret	
coordinate	chief	
condemn	chafe	

cchandeliermsahc

ocylinderlusnocl

rtcocnocqcompeli

rcoincidezcitewq

ecreateqclaretuu

scoordinatepoqwe

pxbqwesohchafepa

ozcondemnfeihclr

ncrescendocarold

doconstituentqua

nocommitteeehcac

tcatastrophesamm

D

dachshund	deceitful	deference
daiquiri	deceive	deferment
daredevil	decided	deferred
daughter	decimal	definite
deacon	dedicate	deign
deadline	deductible	delectable
dealt	defense	delicacy
debtor	defer	delicious

delineate
deluge
deluxe
denizen
deodorant
dependable
dependent
descend
desert (arid land; just reward)
desperate
dessert (sweet at end of meal)
deteriorate
detriment
devastate
devour
diagnose
dialogue *or* dialog

diaphragm
diarrhea
diastolic
dictionary
diphtheria
diplomacy
dirndl
disagree
disappear
disassemble
discipline
discomfit
discreet (showing good judgment)
discrete (separate)
disillusion
disk *or* disc
disparage
dispel

dispelled
dispense
dissatisfied
dissect
dissemble
disseminate
dissent
dissociate
distil *or* distill
distinct
disturb
domicile
donor
dough
drinkable
drought
drudgery
dysentery

My Favorite Spelling Demons That Start with D

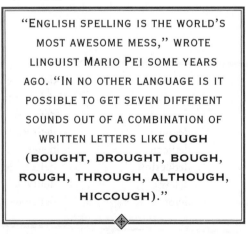

"ENGLISH SPELLING IS THE WORLD'S MOST AWESOME MESS," WROTE LINGUIST MARIO PEI SOME YEARS AGO. "IN NO OTHER LANGUAGE IS IT POSSIBLE TO GET SEVEN DIFFERENT SOUNDS OUT OF A COMBINATION OF WRITTEN LETTERS LIKE **OUGH** (BOUGHT, DROUGHT, BOUGH, ROUGH, THROUGH, ALTHOUGH, HICCOUGH)."

DO THE RIGHT THING

Select the correctly spelled word in each line.

1. diagnose	defferrment	detor
2. diaphragm	delcious	disentery
3. delt	dachshund	daquiri
4. diskrete	delacacy	diplomacy
5. dictionary	delectible	drugery
6. decon	douhg	diphtheria
7. diarrhea	dissturb	devestate
8. drinkeable	dicomfit	devour
9. diegn	daughter	disect
10. disatisfied	diastolic	drouht

ANSWERS

1. diagnose
2. diaphragm
3. dachshund
4. diplomacy
5. dictionary
6. diphtheria
7. diarrhea
8. devour
9. daughter
10. diastolic

E

eatable	emend	enlarge
ecstasy	emigrate	enroll *or* enrol
edible	eminent	enthrall *or* enthral
eighth	emperor	entrepreneur
effect (bring about)	emphasis	enumerate
efficient	emphasize	envelop (to enclose)
elicit	empty	envelope (container for
eligible	enclose	a letter)
elude	encompass	enzyme
emanate	encyclopedia	ephemeral
embarrass	endorsement	Episcopal

Episcopalian
episode
esthetic *or* aesthetic
estimate
et cetera
euphemism
evangelism
exacerbate
exaggerate
exceed
excel
excelled
except (leave out)
excerpt
excitable
excite
excitement
exercise
exhilarate
exorbitant
exorcise
expel
expelled
expense
experiential
extol *or* extoll
extracurricular
extravagant
eyeteeth

My Favorite Spelling Demons That Start with E

_____

_____

_____

_____

_____

_____

X MARKS THE SPOT

Place an X in the space next to each word that is not spelled correctly.

_____ 1. expell
_____ 2. enzyme
_____ 3. estasy
_____ 4. exorbitant
_____ 5. encyclopedia
_____ 6. excitmant
_____ 7. elicit
_____ 8. ephemral
_____ 9. entrepreneur
_____ 10. enumerate
_____ 11. exilarate
_____ 12. efficient
_____ 13. excite
_____ 14. edible
_____ 15. experiental
_____ 16. expense
_____ 17. expeled
_____ 18. eighth
_____ 19. exercise
_____ 20. eateable

ANSWERS

X   1. expell (correct: expel)
    2. enzyme
X   3. estasy (correct: ecstasy)
    4. exorbitant
    5. encyclopedia
X   6. excitment (correct: excitement)
    7. elicit
X   8. ephemral (correct: ephemeral)
    9. entrepreneur
    10. enumerate
X   11. exilarate (correct: exhilarate)
    12. efficient
    13. excite
    14. edible
X   15. experiental (correct: experiential)
    16. expense
X   17. expeled (correct: expelled)
    18. eighth
    19. exercise
X   20. eateable (correct: eatable)

F

fabricate
facade
facile
facsimile
factor
Fahrenheit
faint
fair
fallacy
fallible
falsify
familiar
fare
farther
farthest
fascinate
fashionable
father
favorable
faze
feasible
February
feint
feminine
ferocious
festival
fiancée (engaged woman)
fiancé (engaged man)
fickle
fierce
fiery
finagle
finesse
firsthand
first-rate
flabbergast
flaccid

flakey or flaky
flamboyant
flammable
fledgling
flexible
flimsy
flippant
floppy disk
florescent (flowering)
flourish
fluctuate
fluent
fluorescent
focus
foliage
font
foolhardy
foreign
forbear (leave alone)
forebear
forebode
forecast
foreclose
forefront
foreign
foreknowledge
forensic
foresee

foresight
foretell
foreword (book introduction)
forfeit
formidable
forsake
forsythia
fort
forte (loud musical passage)
fortress
forty
forward
foul (objectionable)
fowl (bird)
franchise
fraudulent
fricassee
frivolous
frontispiece
fulfill
fullness
furniture
further
furthest
futile

My Favorite Spelling Demons That Start with F

_____

_____

_____

_____

_____

_____

FRANKS A LOT

Spell each of the following words correctly. Write your answers in the spaces provided.

1. fricase

2. fortell

3. forfiet

4. fascile

5. fasimile

6. feasable

7. Febuary

8. fallable

9. frontpiece

10. Fahrienheit

ANSWERS

1. fricassee
2. foretell
3. forfeit
4. facile
5. facsimile

6. feasible
7. February
8. fallible
9. frontispiece
10. Fahrenheit

G

gallery	genuine	gnaw
galvanize	gestate	gorgeous
gaseous	ghastly	gorilla
gasoline	ghetto	graduate
gauche	gibe (to tease)	grammar
gauge	gigantic	granary
genealogy	glamorous	grandeur
generic	glimpse	gravitate
generous	glossary	Grecian
genetics	gnarl	grievous

grip
gripe
grippe (influenza)
grotesque
group
grudge
gruesome
guarantee
guaranteed
guaranty
guard
guerrilla
guess
guidance
gullible
guttural
gymnasium

My Favorite Spelling Demons That Start with G

_____

_____

_____

_____

_____

_____

_____

GO, TEAM

Test your ability to spell tricky words that begin with "g." Draw a line from the incorrect spelling to the correct one. Good luck!

1. genune	gruesome
2. gasaline	guaranteed
3. granduer	glamorous
4. geneology	gullible
5. getto	gorgeous
6. guttaral	gauge
7. gramar	ghastly
8. garanteed	gauche
9. guage	gasoline
10. goregous	ghetto
11. gastly	guttural
12. guallable	genealogy
13. glamoros	genuine
14. guache	grammar
15. gruseome	grandeur

H

habeas corpus	height	horde (huge group)
habitant	heinous	hospitable
hobbun	heir	hostile
hail	hemisphere	hullabaloo
hair	hemorrhage	human
hale	hemorrhoid	humane
hallucinate	heresy	humorous
handicap	heritage	hurricane
handicapped	heroes	hydraulic
handkerchief	hesitate	hygiene
handyman	heyday	hymn
hangar	hiatus	hyperbole
hanger	hierarchy	hypocrisy
harangue	hilarious	hypocrite
harass	histrionic	hypothesis
harbor	hoard (save)	hypothetical
hare	holiday	hysteria
hassle	holocaust	
headache	homage	
heaviness	homicide	
hegemony	hoodwink	

My Favorite Spelling Demons That Start with H

_____

_____

_____

_____

_____

_____

_____

Ho-Ho-Ho

Select the correctly spelled word in each line.

1. heyday	herasy	hulabalo
2. hilarious	heirarchy	histeria
3. histrionic	heavyness	homacide
4. hassle	hypacrite	hipothesis
5. handkerchief	hieght	holacaust
6. hegemony	hesatate	hier
7. habitant	hygeine	hymm
8. handicap	hienous	hydralic
9. headache	harrangue	hyparbole
10. heroes	harras	heratage

ANSWERS

1. heyday	6. hegemony
2. hilarious	7. habitant
3. histrionic	8. handicap
4. hassle	9. headache
5. handkerchief	10. heroes

I

icicle
icing
icy
identical
ideology
idle (not active)
idol (object of worship)
idyll (literary form)
ignite
illegally
illegible
illegitimate
illicit
Illinois
illogical
illuminate
illusion
imbroglio
immaculate
immanent
immigrate
imminent
immovable
impartial
impassable (cannot be passed)
impasse
impassible (not able to feel)
impeccable
impede
implacable
implement
implicit
impromptu
impugn
impunity

inaccessible
inaccurate
inadequate
inadmissible
inadvertent
inadvisable
inaudible
incapacitate
incendiary
incessant
inchoate
incident
incite
incommunicable
incommunicado
incredible
indecent
indefinite
independent
inedible
ineffective
inept
inevitable
infallible
inflexible

ingredient
inherent
initiative
innards
innuendo
insight
install
instantaneous
instead
insurance
integrate
intercede
interfere
intimate
intrigue
irascible
irreversible
irrevocable
irritate
inland
Israel
isthmus
it's
its

My Favorite Spelling Demons That Start with I

_____

_____

_____

_____

_____

_____

_____

_____

_____

ME, MYSELF, AND I!

Let's see how well you've learned to spell some intimidating "i" words. Write the correct spelling next to each of the misspelled words below. Then check your spellings against the words in the answer box. If you got all or most of them right, stand up and take a bow. Unless you're already standing.

instantanous _____

inite _____

iciy _____

imaculate _____

impeade _____

inacurate _____

irascable _____

idel _____

instaed _____

impase _____

impartail _____

idolog _____

ANSWERS

instantaneous
ignite
icy
immaculate
impede
inaccurate
irascible
idle
instead
impasse
impartial
ideology

J

jamboree
janitor
jasmine
jeopardy
jodhpur
journal
journeying
juvenile

My Favorite Spelling Demons That Start with J

_____

_____

_____

_____

_____

_____

_____

_____

_____

_____

K

My Favorite Spelling Demons That Start with K

kamikaze

karate

keenness

Keogh

Kewpie

khaki

kilobyte

kilogram

kilometer

kindergartner

kindliness

kiosk

kitsch

knapsack

knead

knickknack

knowledge

knowledgeable

kowtow

kudos

KWICK KWIZ

Spell each of the following words correctly. Write your answers in the space provided.

1. kaki

2. kindlness

3. kotow

4. napsack

5. knowledgable

6. keeness

7. koisk

8. knicknack

9. kamakaze

10. kindgartner

ACCORDING TO AN ARTICLE IN A TORONTO NEWSPAPER, A WOMAN NAMED MARIE CONNOLLY PRESENTED TO A TELLER AT A TORONTO BANK A NOTE THAT READ: "GIVE ME THE MONEY. I'M ARMED AND DANGEROUSE." THE ROBBER MADE OFF WITH $600, BUT DETECTIVES REMEMBERED A SIMILAR ROBBERY THE WEEK BEFORE IN WHICH **DANGEROUS** HAD BEEN SIMILARLY MISSPELLED. USING THIS INFORMATION, POLICE ARRESTED CONNOLLY AND CHARGED HER WITH COMMITTING THE EARLIER ROBBERY. SEE HOW IMPORTANT SPELLING IS?

L

label	laryngitis	leisure
laboratory	laudable	length
labyrinth	laughable	lenient
lacerate	lavatory	lesser
lackadaisical	lead	lessor
laid	led	lettuce
laissez-faire	ledger	leverage
laminate	legend	liable
landscape	legible	libel
larceny	legitimate	library

license	liqueur (sweet liquor)	lose
lieutenant	liquor (alcoholic drink)	lounge
lightening	literacy	loup
lightning	litigate	lovable
limousine	loath (reluctant)	luau
linear	loathe (hate)	luncheon
lingerie	loiter	
linguist	loose	
liniment	loquacious	

My Favorite Spelling Demons That Start with L

_____

_____

_____

_____

_____

_____

"LITE" AND LO-CAL

Cross out the misspelled word in each line. Spell the word correctly on the line provided.

1. label	laryngitis	laudable	liqor
2. lunchon	lacerate	lead	legible
3. legitimate	lettuce	liable	laughble
4. legder	legend	leverage	license
5. libel	lackadasical	litigate	lieutenant
6. liesure	lesser	luau	lingerie
7. laid	lavatory	limosine	linguist

8. laminate	linear	labratory	loiter
9. labrinth	led	length	lounge
10. larceny	landscape	lenient	libbery

Answers

1. liquor
2. luncheon
3. laughable
4. ledger
5. lackadaisical
6. leisure
7. limousine
8. laboratory
9. labyrinth
10. library

M

macabre
macaroon
machination
mademoiselle
maggoty
magnanimous
magnate (business person)
magnet
maintain
malaise
malediction
malleable
maneuver
manicotti
manila
mannequin
mansion
manufacture
manuscript

martial
marriage
marquee (a permanent canopy)
marquis (a gem setting)
marmalade
masculine
Massachusetts
material (fabric)
materiel (equipment)
mathematics
mausoleum
maximize
mayonnaise
meant
medal (award)
meddle (interfere)
medicine
medieval
mediocre

Mediterranean
memento
memorabilia
memorable
memorandum
menagerie
mercenary
mere
metal (iron, et al.)
metamorphosis
metaphor
meticulous
mettle (strength)
mezzanine
midget
millennium
milligram
millimeter
miner (person who mines)

miniature	molecule	movable
minor (a youth)	monastery	mucous
minutes	monitor	multinational
misanthrope	monument	municipal
misconstrue	moral (ethical)	muscle (body tissue)
missal (prayer book)	morale (emotional	museum
missile (weapon)	condition)	mussel (mollusk)
Mississippi	morass	muumuu
misspell	morning (dawn)	mystery
misstate	mortgage	mystic
mitigate	mourning (act of	
mnemonic	sorrow)	

My Favorite Spelling Demons That Start with M

_____

_____

_____

_____

_____

_____

MMM MMM GOOD

There are twenty-five spelling words that begin with "m" hidden in this puzzle. To complete the puzzle, locate and circle all the words. The words may be written forward or backward. Good luck!

Here are the words to look for:

macabre	mere	metal
medal	marquis	Massachusetts
memento	midget	mystic
malleable	martial	
Mediterranean	manila	
mezzanine	magnet	
missal	medieval	
mannequin	meant	
marquee	malediction	
miner	mademoiselle	

Massachusettscitsym
pmannequinmeantlrlm
xsiuqramlaitramqqae
zmacabremanilawezvm
emedalmidgetbobrzeo
smarqueemezzanineir
ereotnememmissalzda
aelbaellammagnetzeb
lMediterraneanpopmi
amaledictionminerzl
mmademoisellemetali
merenthaJRozakisppa

ANSWERS

Massachusettscitsym
pmannequinmeantlrlm
xsiuqramlaitramqqae
z**macabremanila**wezvm
emed**almidget**bobrzeo
s**marqueemezzanine**ir
ereotne**memmiss**alzda
a**elbaellammagnet**zeb
l**Mediterranean**popmi
a**maledictionminer**zl
m**mademoisellemet**ali
merentha**JRozakis**ppa

N

napery	nickelodeon
naive	niece
nasal	ninety
nausea	nineteen
naval (ocean-going)	ninth
navel (belly button;	nominate
orange)	nonpareil
necessary	notable
necessitate	noticeable
nemesis	notary
neutral	nuclear
nevertheless	nutrition

My Favorite Spelling Demons That Start with N

NAUGHTY, BUT NICE

Match the incorrectly spelled word with its correctly spelled counterpart. Write the letter of the answer in the space provided.

Incorrectly Spelled	Correctly Spelled
_____1. neice	a. nuclear
_____2. ninteen	b. nasal
_____3. ninty	c. neutral
_____4. nasel	d. niece
_____5. nonpariel	e. necessary
_____6. nasel	f. notable
_____7. nemasis	g. ninth
_____8. nausaa	h. nasal
_____9. napary	i. nemesis
_____10. nuetral	j. naive
_____11. nineth	k. necessitate
_____12. noticable	l. nonpareil
_____13. neverthless	m. nineteen
_____14. niave	n. napery
_____15. notarie	o. nevertheless
_____16. noteable	p. nickelodeon
_____17. nickleodeon	q. ninety
_____18. necessatate	r. nausea
_____19. nuclaer	s. notary
_____20. necassary	t. noticeable

ANSWERS

1. d	6. b	11. g	16. f
2. m	7. i	12. t	17. p
3. q	8. r	13. o	18. k
4. h	9. n	14. j	19. a
5. l	10. c	15. s	20. e

O

obedient	odyssey	opalescent
obeisance	offense	opinion
obese	offish	opponents
obnoxious	often	orphan
obstinate	omelette	oscillate
occasion	omission	ostracize
occupational	omit	oxygen
occupy	onerous	
occurrence	onus	

My Favorite Spelling Demons That Start with O

_____

_____

_____

_____

_____

_____

A, B, C . . . 1, 2, 3

Here's a painless and effective way to memorize the spelling of a group of words: Place them in alphabetical order. Below is a list of fifteen words that begin with the letter "o." Alphabetize the words and rewrite them in order.

ostracize	1.	
onerous	2.	
omission	3.	
oxygen	4.	
odyssey	5.	
offish	6.	
offense	7.	
occurrence	8.	

oscillate	9.
occasion	10.
obeisance	11.
opinion	12.
omelette	13.
opalescent	14.
obnoxious	15.

ANSWERS

1. obeisance	6. offense	11. opalescent
2. obnoxious	7. offish	12. opinion
3. occasion	8. omelette	13. oscillate
4. occurrence	9. omission	14. ostracize
5. odyssey	10. onerous	15. oxygen

P

pacify	passable	phenomena (singular)
pacarr	pastime	phenomenon (plural)
pageant	patina	philanthropy
paid	patriot	Philippines
palate (roof of the mouth)	paucity	physique
	peccadillo	picador
palette (artist's tool)	peer (equal or stare)	pier (dock)
pallet (mattress)	penance	pigeon
pamphlet	pendant (ornament)	pillar
pantomime	pendent (hanging)	pimento
papal	penetrate	pimentos
parachute	penicillin	pique
parallel	peninsula	piranha
paralysis	perceive	placate
parasite	perennial	plankton
pare (to cut)	permanence	plateau
pari-mutuel	pertain	plausible
parliament	petite	playwright
parochial	pharmacy	pledge
parole	phase	pneumatics

pneumonia

pogrom

poignant

polarize

possess

prairie

precede (come before)

precedent

preeminent

preempt

premier (first)

premiere (first performance)

prerequisite

prerogative

prescribe

presence

president

pretty

prevail

principal (head of school, money)

principle (rule)

proceed (continue)

procession

procrastinate

prologue

prominent

pronounce

pronunciation

prophet

proscribe (forbid)

proxy

pseudonym

psychiatry

psychology

psychedelic

punctual

punctuate

My Favorite Spelling Demons That Start with P

_____

_____

_____

_____

_____

_____

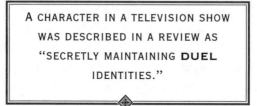

A CHARACTER IN A TELEVISION SHOW WAS DESCRIBED IN A REVIEW AS "SECRETLY MAINTAINING **DUEL** IDENTITIES."

PICK 'N' PLAY

Place an "X" next to each word that is not spelled correctly.

_____ 1. parliament

_____ 2. pilar

_____ 3. pneumonia

_____ 4. pamplet

_____ 5. pasable

_____ 6. peccadillo
_____ 7. pagant
_____ 8. pari-mutuel
_____ 9. prerequisite
_____ 10. prevale
_____ 11. preminent
_____ 12. Philippines
_____ 13. penansula
_____ 14. proced
_____ 15. pantomime
_____ 16. percieve
_____ 17. pigeon
_____ 18. parol
_____ 19. psuedonym
_____ 20. paean

ANSWERS

1. parliament
X 2. pilar (correct: pillar)
3. pneumonia
X 4. pamplet (correct: pamphlet)
X 5. pasable (correct: passable)
6. peccadillo
X 7. pagant (correct: pageant)
8. pari-mutuel
9. prerequisite
X 10. prevale (correct: prevail)
X 11. preminent (correct: preeminent)
12. Philippines
X 13. penansula (correct: peninsula)
X 14. proced (correct: proceed)
15. pantomime
X 16. percieve (correct: perceive)
17. pigeon
X 18. parol (correct: parole)
X 19. psuedonym (correct: pseudonym)
20. paean

Q

quack	quagga	queasy
quad	qualification	quench
quadrant	quality	quetzal
quadrennial	quantity	queue
quadriceps	quark	quibble
quadrille	quarry	quilt
quadruplet	quartz	quota
quaff	quay	quotation

My Favorite Spelling Demons That Start with Q

_____

_____

_____

_____

_____

OUR DESIRE TO LEARN TO SPELL CORRECTLY IS NOTHING NEW. ONE OF AMERICA'S FIRST BEST-SELLERS WASN'T A ROMANCE, A COOKBOOK, OR EVEN A TRAVEL GUIDE. NOPE, IT WAS THE COUNTRY'S FIRST SPELLING BOOK, NOAH WEBSTER'S **THE AMERICAN SPELLING BOOK.** BY 1818, MORE THAN FIVE MILLION COPIES HAD BEEN SOLD. SIXTEEN YEARS LATER, THE NUMBER WAS UP TO AT LEAST FIFTEEN MILLION. BY THE BEGINNING OF THE CIVIL WAR, 42 MILLION COPIES WERE IN THE HANDS OF AMERICANS EAGER TO LEARN HOW TO SPELL. FROM 1876 TO 1890, MORE THAN 11 MILLION COPIES FLEW OFF THE SHELVES. THIS FIGURE IS EVEN MORE IMPRESSIVE SINCE THERE WERE FEWER THAN 100,000 PEOPLE IN ILLINOIS, AND THE ENTIRE POPULATION OF NEW YORK WAS LESS THAN ONE-THIRD OF THE PRESENT POPULATION OF MANHATTAN.

QUICK AND DIRTY

Supply the missing letter or letters in each word below.

1. q_____ack
2. qui_____ble
3. que_____ sy
4. que_____ e
5. qualif_____ cation
6. quadri_____ le
7. q _____ antity
8. quar_____ y

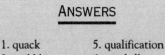

ANSWERS

1. quack	5. qualification
2. quibble	6. quadrille
3. queasy	7. quantity
4. queue	8. quarry

R

rabid
racism
raconteur
radiant
raiment
rancor
rarely
rarity
raspberry
rationale
raucous
ravenous
ravioli
raze (destroy)
reality
rebuttal
rebelled
recede
receipt
receive
recommend
recommit
reconcile
reconnaissance
recreate

recreation
referee
regale
reign (rule)
rein (bridle)
relevance
relief
relieve
reminisce
renaissance
rendezvous
renounce
repeat
repetition
repel
repellent
repent
repentance
repertoire
replace
replacement
requisite
rescue
resister (a person who
  resists)

resistor (electrical
  object)
restaurant
resume (begin again)
résumé (job
  qualifications)
resuscitate
reticent
reveille
reverent
rhapsody
rhyme
rhythm
ricochet
right
riskiness
rite (ceremony)
rogue
rookie
rout (defeat)
route (highway)
rudiment
ruin

My Favorite Spelling Demons That Start with R

_____

_____

_____

_____

_____

AN ESPECIALLY THRILLING TELEVISION SHOW WAS
DESCRIBED IN A REVIEW AS A
"**SEERING** DRAMA."

ROCK AND ROLL

In the following groups of words, one word is misspelled. In each group, select the misspelled word and spell it correctly in the space provided.

1. raconteur
   rebelled   _____
   rasberry
   reconcile

2. repetition
   recieve   _____
   rogue
   recommend

3. ravenous
   relevance   _____
   recomit
   requisite

4. rudiment
   restarant   _____
   ravioli
   rookie

5. resume
   rapsody   _____
   ruin
   replacement

6. rhythm
   rebutal   _____
   reconnaissance
   reality

7. resusitate
   route   _____
   relieve
   reticent

8. radiant _____
   rarity
   refere
   repellent

9. rationale _____
   regale
   rarly
   raucous

10. raiment _____
    racicsm
    ricochet
    rabid

ANSWERS

1. raspberry	6. rebuttal
2. receive	7. resuscitate
3. recommit	8. referee
4. restaurant	9. rarely
5. rhapsody	10. racism

S

sabotage	sapphire	schism
saboteur	sarcasm	science
saccharin (sugar substitute)	sari	scion
	sassafras	scissors
saccharine (sweet)	satellite	scrip (temporary currency)
sacrament	saucer	
sacrifice	sauerbraten	script (writing)
safety	sauerkraut	schnapps
salmon	savior	secede
salon (elegant room)	saxophone	secret
saloon (bar)	scalpel	secrete
sandwich	scarcity	sedentary
sanguine	schedule	seer (prophet)

segregate
seize
semiannual
senate
sensible
separate
sere (withered)
serf (peasant)
sergeant
sew
shear (cut)
sheer (transparent)
shepherd
sheriff
shillelagh
shoulder
shrapnel
silhouette
sincerely
skillful
sleazy
sleigh
smorgasbord
sociable
solace
soldier
solitude
somersault
sooth (truth)
soothe (ease)
sophomore
source
souvenir
sovereign
sow (plant)
spaghetti
speak
speech
spinnaker

sponge
squeamish
squirrel
stamina
stampede
stationary (not moving)
stationery (writing
    paper)
statue
stature
statute
staunch
stereotype
straight
strait
stevedore
strength
strict
suave
subpoena
subsequent
subterranean
subtle

subtlety
subtly
successful
succession
sue
sugar
suit (outfit)
suite (rooms)
summary (précis)
summery (like summer)
supercilious
supersede
superstition
supplement
surf (waves)
surrender
surreptitious
surrogate
suspense
synonym
synthesize
syphilis

My Favorite Spelling Demons That Start with S

_____

_____

_____

_____

_____

REMEMBER THAT ENGLISH IS SPOKEN NOT
ONLY IN THE UNITED STATES AND GREAT
BRITAIN, BUT ALSO IN AUSTRALIA, NEW
ZEALAND, THROUGHOUT AFRICA, THE
INDIAN SUBCONTINENT, AND MANY
ISLANDS. THIS GREATLY AFFECTS THE
PRONUNCIATION OF MANY WORDS.

SHORT AND SWEET

Circle the ten misspelled words in the following passage. Each word will start with "s."

"Sabotage! Who could have imagined a saboteur in our midst!" Mr. Salmon said with an edge of sarcazm in his usually saccarine voice. Gripping the scissors in one hand and the bottle of schnaps in the other, the sedentary scion siezed the moment. "What a sleasy charge!" he said in a supersilious way. "The only thing we can do now is get a sauerbraten and sauerkraut sandwich."

"This will create a scism," the partners muttered. "It could set us way behind scedule unless we are skillfull in our dealings with the sheriff." With that, they left for the salon to be sociable, watch satallite TV, and enjoy some delicious sassafras tea.

ANSWERS

1. sarcasm	6. supercilious
2. saccharine	7. schism
3. schnapps	8. schedule
4. seized	9. skillful
5. sleazy	10. satellite

T

tacit	tenure	threshold
taciturn	territory	through
tangible	tête-à-tête	thwart
taught (past tense of to teach)	their (possessive)	tolerant
	themselves	tomorrow
taut (tight)	there (place)	tonsil
taxable	thermometer	tort (wrongful act)
technique	thesaurus	torte (dessert)
teenage	they're (contraction for they are)	torturous
teepee		toupee
temperature	though	toxic
tenuous	thought	traceable

traitor
traitorous
transcend
transient
trapeze
trauma
traveler
treachery
traveling
trellis
troop (soldiers)
trouble
troupe (performers)
turkeys
turquoise
twelfth
tyranny

My Favorite Spelling Demons That Start with T

_____

_____

_____

_____

_____

_____

_____

_____

_____

_____

> IF WE SIMPLIFIED SPELLING, WORDS SUCH
> AS **NIGHT** AND **KNIGHT**, **SON** AND
> **SUN**, **BARE** AND **BEAR** WOULD NO
> LONGER BE DIFFERENTIATED.

T FOR TWO

In the space provided, write **T** if the word is spelled correctly or **F** if it is misspelled.

_____	1. tacit	_____	11. temperature
_____	2. transeint	_____	12. tyranny
_____	3. technique	_____	13. themselfs
_____	4. thesarus	_____	14. twelfth
_____	5. tenure	_____	15. taxeable
_____	6. trechery	_____	16. turquoise
_____	7. traveling	_____	17. territory
_____	8. turkies	_____	18. trouble
_____	9. trellis	_____	19. tenuouos
_____	10. thier	_____	20. teenage

ANSWERS

___T___	1. tacit
___F___	2. transient
___T___	3. technique
___F___	4. thesaurus
___T___	5. tenure
___F___	6. treachery
___T___	7. traveling
___F___	8. turkeys
___T___	9. trellis
___F___	10. their
___T___	11. temperature
___T___	12. tyranny
___F___	13. themselves
___T___	14. twelfth
___F___	15. taxable
___T___	16. turquoise
___T___	17. territory
___T___	18. trouble
___F___	19. tenuous
___T___	20. teenage

U

ubiquitous
ukulele
ultimatum
umbrella
unanimity
uncommitted
underrate

unforgettable
unique
unnecessary
unoccupied
unparalleled
unprecedented
unpredictable

unsuccessful
until
unwieldy
urban (city)
urbane (witty)

My Favorite Spelling Demons That Start with U

_____
_____
_____
_____
_____
_____
_____

U CAN DO IT!

Spell each of the following words correctly. Then create a mnemonic (memory device) to help you remember each word. Try using songs, stressed letters, or rhymes.

Misspelled Word	Correct Spelling and Mnemonic
1. ubiqitous	
2. unparaleled	
3. uncomitted	
4. underate	
5. unforgetable	
6. unweildy	

ANSWERS

1. ubiquitous
2. unparalleled
3. uncommitted

4. underrate
5. unforgettable
6. unwieldy

V

vacation	vellum	vindictive
vaccinate	velocity	violate
vacillate	vengeance	violent
vaqueros	verbatim	virile
vacuum	verbiage	vis-à-vis
vague	verisimilitude	visible
valedictory	vertical	vitamin
variable	veterinary	vociferous
various	viand	voluble
vegetable	vichyssoise	voyeur
veil	vicious	
vein	view	

My Favorite Spelling Demons That Start with V

_____

_____

_____

_____

_____

_____

_____

V Is for Victory

Cross out the misspelled word in each line. Then spell the word correctly on the line provided.

1. vacuum	valedictory	visable	
2. view	vien	vacillate	
3. velocity	veterinary	verbage	
4. voilent	violate	vicious	
5. viel	vaporous	vitamin	
6. various	vacinate	vociferous	
7. voyeur	vegetable	verticle	
8. velum	verisimilitude	voluble	
9. viand	vage	verbatim	
10. vichyssoise	virile	vacaition	

ANSWERS

1. visible	6. vaccinate
2. vein	7. vertical
3. verbiage	8. vellum
4. violent	9. vague
5. veil	10. vacation

W

waist (midsection)	wear (attire)	wield
waive (renounce, relinquish)	wealth	willpower
	wean	witch
waiver	weather	wittingly
wallpaper	week (seven days)	wondrous
ware (item for sale)	weigh (balance)	workable
warfare	weird	worrisome
warrior	welfare	wraith
washable	where (place)	wreath (noun)
waste (throw away)	wherever	wreathe (verb)
wave (surf, breaker)	whet	wreck
waver	whether	wrestle
weak (not strong)	wholly	wretch

My Favorite Spelling Demons That Start with W

_____

_____

_____

_____

WHICH WITCH IS WHICH?

Spell the "w" words that match each definition.

Definition   **W Word**

1. attire   _____

2. item for sale   _____

3. place   _____

4. relinquish   _____

5. breaker   _____

6. fragile, delicate   _____

7. seven days   _____

8. throw away   _____

9. midsection of the body   _____

10. balance   _____

ANSWERS

1. wear	6. weak
2. ware	7. week
3. where	8. waste
4. waive	9. waist
5. wave	10. weigh

Y

My Favorite Spelling Demons That Start with Y

yacht
yogurt or yoghurt
your (possessive)
you're (contraction
  for *you are*)

Z

My Favorite Spelling Demons That Start with Z

zeal
zealot
zeppelin
zoology
zucchini